practice
practice

ashton hamm

practice practice

Edited by
peggy deamer and dariel cobb

ORO
EDITIONS
Novato, California

Contents

Preface

When I began studying architecture at Virginia Tech in 2009, I never thought I'd be interested in the technical and formal configurations of architecture firms as legal entity types, nor did I acknowledge how deeply the collaborative ethos of the Bauhaus pedagogy had been embedded in my understanding of architecture and how to co-create it. In understanding how important collaboration was to me, yet how rarely it felt acknowledged and welcomed in the profession, a realization started to come together—that traditional methods of practice (structurally and emotionally) are not cohesive to co-creating architecture. I knew that alternative models existed, but I didn't understand the details of their inner workings. Now that I've been through the process of creating an architectural cooperative and have spoken to many who are interested in the model, I feel that this information needs to be easier to access. This is what compelled me to begin working on this book.

I initially encountered the cooperative model as a structural strategy for an architectural firm during a professional practice course in my fifth year at Virginia Tech. The course, titled "Designing Practice," required students to build out the details of their "dream firm," complete with monthly income statements and balance sheets. Though the assignment was brief, I was intrigued. At that time, I had been engaged in design projects (posters, competitions, etc.) with a cohort of friends. My "dream firm" became a cooperative with them—UXO.

After leaving school, my cohort began separate professional paths in different cities but continued to work together on competitions after hours. Simultaneously, we were getting involved with our local chapters of The Architecture Lobby, an organization advocating for fair labor and wage practices within the profession. Eventually it was time to leave traditional employment and start UXO. I started alone at first to test the waters: Is there work? Can I do this? What is it like to not have a boss? About 1.5 years in, I found there was enough work to ask one of the original UXO members to join. It was happening! By that point we were both very involved in The Architecture Lobby, which had begun to sow the seeds of cooperative practice in architecture firms. For us, the cooperative entity provided a structural way to ensure equality among workers and ensure that true collaboration was written into our bylaws. The cooperative model we wanted would structurally reinforce collaboration through shared ownership— we wanted more than merely an ethos of cooperation or a rhetoric of collectivity. At this point we were licensed, too, so UXO became uxo architects—attempting to emphasize that multiple architects lead the firm, without associating anyone's last name.

Needing to incorporate, we chose to do so as an architectural cooperative, learning in the process that we were the first of our kind in California. It took about one year and two rejections from the California secretary of state to realize the process was more complicated than we had imagined. Since architecture practices in California are unable to use the cooperative corporation statute, we chose a more traditional entity, the S Corporation, and tailored our bylaws to encourage cooperative values as much as possible within its legal constraints. (More on this in chapter 3.) We saw other young firms around us defaulting to traditional business entities and bylaws, never looking at them again, so we felt that building our practice as a legal entity was one of our projects. For us, the bylaws were and are a living project that we continually modify as we learn from the operations of our firm. We wanted to practice *practice*.

This experience made me realize how opaque the process of incorporating as a cooperative is for any interested architect. I got more involved with The Architecture Lobby's Cooperative Network working group, which advocates for the proliferation of architectural cooperatives among small firms, whether they are worker-owned like uxo or function as networks between firms to share purchasing and marketing power and/or workers. I also became increasingly involved with the larger worker-cooperative movement, amazed by how robust of an ecosystem it is.

In 2018, I was awarded the Donald and Joanna Sunshine Architecture Fellow Alumni Award from Virginia Tech, which I used to interview twenty-eight small architecture firms in Spain and California. I was familiar with, and saw similarities between, the architecture scene in both places, having spent a year of my education at the Escuela Tecnica Superior de Arquitectura de Madrid (ETSAM). I had been practicing in California for about four years at that point. I wanted to learn the nuts and bolts of firm management, things that aren't normally discussed in the office or studio. How are they organized? How are they getting projects? What is driving those flashy images on a firm's website? How did they make it through the Great Recession? What is their internal hierarchy? Do they want to grow? I came away with consistent evidence that small offices are struggling. Firms which had been around for years and barely survived the Great Recession watched many of their friends' offices collapse. Younger firms described myriad strategies to keep their practice afloat. While I wasn't specifically seeking cooperative or non-cooperative firms, in hindsight I recognized how the model, especially in the form of a cooperative network, could benefit such firms.

More recently, both as part of The Architecture Lobby and as an individual, I've met with other small offices interested in the cooperative model. Whether or not any end up adopting the model, I have learned a great deal about the legal components of the cooperative structure and the ethos of the firms that seek them out. That information should not stop with me. My goal is to bring part of the vital co-op spirit from small businesses across the United States into the world of architectural practice.

Acknowledgments

I'd like to thank the following people for participating in this long journey:

Peggy Deamer
Dariel Cobb
Therese Tuttle of Tuttle Law Group
South Mountain Company
Ryan Rose of Capital Bookkeeping Cooperative
The COOP Network Working Group of The Architecture Lobby
Dan Bergs of Wegner CPAs
Jason Wiener of Jason Wiener | p.c.
Jason Geils of Flora Design Cooperative
Meegan Moriarty of the USDA
Matthew Ridgeway
Alice Armstrong
Megan McAllister
Palmyra Geraki
Manuel Shvartzberg
Hilary Byron
Frank Weiner
Dan Hemmendinger
James Heard
Chelsea Kilburn

Introduction

The business of architecture—shaped by antitrust legislation and pro-corporate government policies—has created an extractive, inequitable, and precarious environment for its practitioners. The pressures of capitalism have led many small firms, which make up roughly three quarters of architecture offices in the United States, to adopt diverse and ad hoc organizational and survival strategies. For architecture practitioners, the result is long hours, low wages, fluctuating deadlines, and undefined job descriptions. Worker cooperatives offer a solution: a structure for practice that is equitable, democratic, and empowering.

There are several types of cooperatives: consumer, producer, worker, purchasing, and multi-stakeholder.[1] Consumer cooperatives are owned by the consumers who buy from the co-op entity, thereby cutting out the cost of the middle-man retailer. This includes grocery coops, credit unions, and retail co-ops like REI. Producer cooperatives are owned by producers of goods, and the cooperative is a means to reach a larger market. Ocean Spray, Organic Valley, and Cabot Cheese are all producer cooperatives. Worker cooperatives are owned by workers, giving them democratic access to governance and financial control of the company. Equal Exchange, Union Cab Cooperative, and Cooperative Home Care Associates are examples of worker cooperatives. Purchasing cooperatives allow organizations or businesses to partner and combine purchasing power for better prices. Ace Hardware is an example of a purchasing cooperative. A multi-stakeholder cooperative is a hybrid form wherein owners can benefit from multiple co-op types. This book primarily examines the worker cooperative.

Worker-owned architectural cooperatives are few and far between. Today, there are only twelve architectural firms that identify as cooperatives in the United States. Indeed, the idea of cooperation is antithetical to the current profession of architecture, which was founded on exclusion, elitism, and exceptionalism. The insulation of architects as a professional class has heightened their precarity, alienated workers, and bred toxic work environments. The irony is that architecture, like other design professions, naturally lends itself to the cooperative model: it engages a complex web of actors with tasks that must be coordinated for project delivery. Authorship belongs not just to the firm owners whose names adorn a firm's front door, but also to the many actors involved in the realization of the project. However, cooperatives have yet to infiltrate white collar industries. Many state incorporation laws obscure pathways for cooperative incorporation of professional industries, and the variation of laws between different states amplifies confusion and diminishes interest.

6   To better understand the work-arounds necessary for architectural cooperatives to function, the evolving trajectories of both worker cooperatives and the profession of architecture will be examined in parallel. Cooperatives have a tumultuous history that has largely followed the struggles of the labor movement; architects have fought to distinguish themselves from the working class and thus distanced themselves from pro-labor movements. Part 1 of this book is divided into three sections. The first offers a synopsis of cooperatives and their place in labor-forward movements; the second examines the professionalization of architecture and its conscious distancing from laborer status; and the third offers an overview of moments when worker-forward organizations intersect with the practice of architecture and lend proof of concept. Part 2 focuses on possible legal frameworks, including the tax code, and offers a practical guide to starting an architectural cooperative. It outlines the nuts and bolts of cooperativizing architecture firms, both worker-owned and networked. Part 3 is an interview with several owners of South Mountain Company, an architectural and building cooperative based in Martha's Vineyard, Massachusetts, founded in 1975. The appendix includes a glossary of terms and incorporation resources such as sample bylaws. While there are many resources available concerning worker cooperatives, I have tried to reference those that I found helpful during uxo's incorporation process.

Chapter 1:
A Brief Synopsis of Co-Ops

The worker-cooperative model has a tenuous history in the United States. Fueled by a free-market political economy, worker cooperatives have effectively been designed out of existence. To succeed at all, the model has had to obscure itself into a capitalist frame of reference. Many attorneys, accountants, and financial institutions are not familiar with the cooperative model.[2] Hence, I've provided some background.

It is important to understand the ideological and historical origins of the concept of cooperatives—associated politically with anarchism—and its fractious relationship with socialism and unionism. The cooperative movement, in its modern form as a political/economic ideology, begins in the mid-nineteenth century with French philosopher and economist Pierre-Joseph Proudhon, the so-called father of anarchism, and his endorsement of cooperatives. Proudhon believed that the small producer co-ops of Europe could help usher in the anti-monarchial revolution that would come to pass in 1848: "This role [of workers' companies] will above all consist in the management of the great instruments of labor and of certain tasks, which 'demand' both a great division of functions and a great collective force."[3] At the end of his life, however, he admitted that the cooperative movement had not developed as he had hoped.

Russian political philosopher Mikhail Bakunin picked up on Proudhon's campaign and led the anarchist/cooperative faction of the International Workingmen's Association (IWA).[4] At the 1872 Hague Congress, the fifth assembly of the IWA, Bakunin's faction argued for the replacement of the state by federations of self-governing communes, an idea contrary to the imagination of Karl Marx, who argued that only the state itself—controlled directly by the proletariat—could bring about socialism. Marx called the commune supporters, "the socialist bourgeoise," who "want all the advantages of modern social conditions without the struggles and dangers necessarily resulting therefrom. They desire the existing state of society minus its revolutionary and disintegrating elements."[5] As Bakunin was unable to attend the Hague Congress, Marxist ideology carried the day.

Following the Russian Revolution, the role of private profits in cooperatives, in which profit is shared internally but generally not state controlled, made them politically problematic in Russia and communist Europe alike. As Vladimir Lenin wrote in 1921:

> The ideas at the bottom [of Bakunin's producer coops] are radically wrong in theory. ... First, the concept "producer" combines proletarians with semi-proletarians

and small commodity producers, thus radically departing from the fundamental concept of the class struggle and from the fundamental demand that a precise distinction be drawn between classes. ... Secondly, the bidding for or flirtation with the non-Party masses ... is an equally radical departure from Marxism.[6]

As socialist philosopher Rosa Luxemburg explains:

The workers forming a co-operative in the field of production are ... faced with the contradictory necessity of governing themselves with the utmost absolutism. They are obliged to take toward themselves the role of capitalist entrepreneur—a contradiction that accounts for the usual failure of production co-operatives which either become pure capitalist enterprises or, if the workers' interests continue to predominate, end by dissolving.[7]

Despite seemingly intractable positions on the revolutionary credentials of co-ops, compromises inevitably emerged. By 1923, Lenin viewed cooperatives "with state supervision and control" as essential tools for educating Russian peasants on trading power post revolution. He identified them as the best vehicle to establish a real and proper socialist order.[8] Lenin's successor Joseph Stalin was always in favor of state ownership of the means of production, yet Stalin's five-year plan likewise encouraged the replacement of individual peasant farms by collectives to increase food supplies for growing urban populations and for export. By the 1980s, in the era of Soviet perestroika, cooperatives flourished. In 1985, the cooperative sector of the Soviet economy was comprised of some 26,000 collective farms supporting 12.7 million workers.[9]

In the United States, where free-market capitalism did not leave space to concern oneself with the ideological fractures between European socialists, cooperatives originally worked hand in hand with trade unions. In 1834, unions from across the United States came together to form their own labor federation, the National Trades' Union (NTU), which in turn supported at least eighteen production cooperatives under its representational umbrella.[10] Disbanded in 1837, it was followed by the National Labor Union (NLU), a similar federation of workers' movements in 1866. William Sylvis, a co-founder of the NLU, believed that "the time has come when we should abandon the whole system of strikes and make cooperation the foundation of our organization and the prime object of all our efforts."[11]

Shortly thereafter, in 1869, the Knights of Labor formed, which would briefly become the largest labor organization in the world. The Knights envisioned a "cooperative commonwealth," a widespread economic democracy brought about through a union of cooperatives. Their membership crossed race and gender lines and included both skilled and unskilled labor. When the Knights were unjustly blamed for the Haymarket Riot in Chicago—a violent conflict sprung from the confrontation between workers striking for an eight-hour workday and the Chicago Police Department, during which a bomb was detonated—public mistrust led to a decline in their membership. The Knights' involvement was never proven.[12] Precipitated by the Knights' decline, the American Federation of Labor (AFL) was founded in 1886, representing several national craft unions, and soon gained prominence. Taking a more conservative approach to the scope of unionization, it focused mainly on working conditions and workers' immediate demands rather than devising a long-term strategy to challenge the structure underpinning capitalist ownership of the means of production. Unlike the Knights, the AFL did not support cooperatives. Historian and activist John Curl describes the reasons underpinning the AFL's posture:

> They were against worker cooperatives not only because of past failures, but also because cooperatives were associated with radicalism and radical movements, of which they wanted no part, and because cooperatives obscured the line between employee and employer. This confused the union's role as bargaining agent, which they saw as the union's basic identity, with the contract the eternal goal.[13]

In the systemic the shift from craft-based work to mechanized industrialization, the Congress of Industrial Organizations (CIO) challenged the AFL's hegemony and its insistence on separating workers by craft or trade. Originally created as a committee within the AFL, the CIO formed in 1935 after a group of industrial unions were expelled from the organization. This group coalesced around John L. Lewis, a member of the United Mine Workers (UMW), who had fought for laborers in the automotive and rubber industries. The CIO became a strong and combative rival of the AFL. However, most of the critical tensions that once separated the two organizations eased after the AFL not only embraced industrial organizing during World War II, but also included industrial unions in its membership. The combined AFL-CIO was formed in 1955 as the dominant labor organization in the United States. The rise of industrial unions deflected attention away from cooperatives, which developed along a separate trajectory.

Cooperatives have historical ebbs and flows distinct from their association with labor unions. Traditionally, craft industries have been organized under the "master-apprentice" model in which everyone was considered a worker. When employers began exploiting labor to make more profit, cooperatives were identified as a vehicle to combat inequality in the wage employment system prevalent in the early nineteenth century.[14] Cooperatives were leveraged by both independent workers and employees to fight for their autonomy and take ownership of their labor.[15]

The post-Civil War period was a productive one for cooperatives in many industries and very significant for newly freed Black Americans.[16] By 1863, the UK-founded Rochdale cooperatives and those based on their principles emerged in the United States and began to attract interest from within the American labor movement.[17] By the early 1870s, hundreds of cooperatives were founded, and by the 1880s, an estimated 334 worker cooperatives were formed.[18]

The Sherman Antitrust Act of 1890, which prohibited activities that restricted competition and interstate commerce, effected both unions and co-ops. The Sherman Act, which would eventually target and bust the corporations monopolizing meat packing and meat distribution,[19] was initially used as a tool for union busting and outlawing cooperatives, rather than regulating trusts between big businesses. The Sherman Act "made numerous types of cooperatives illegal and was used to break strikes twelve times in ten years, yet never to break a trust."[20]

Many cooperatives and unions succumbed to the pressures of enforced anti-competition clauses instituted by the Sherman Act.

In 1914, Congress passed the Clayton Antitrust Act and further defined and prohibited monopolies, banning price discrimination and anti-competitive mergers. The Clayton Act, in an about-face from its purported anti-union stance, made unions legal under federal law. It provided exemptions for producer organizations from antitrust laws and allowed for the formation of agricultural cooperatives. It was the first piece of legislation to exempt farmers from antitrust laws. However, because the language of the act was weak and vague, it failed to create adequate protections. Representative Andrew Volstead, a republican from Minnesota, led the charge to rethink the Clayton Act. He and his supporters drafted additional legislation using the Rochdale Cooperative principles as a reference. The Capper-Volstead Act of 1922 fully sanctioned agricultural cooperatives, granting these businesses exemptions from antitrust legislation. It defined an explicit exemption from antitrust legislation for producer cooperatives, specified the structure of an organization necessary to qualify for the exemption, and described the activities in which the organization could participate.[21] By 1939, half the farms in the US belonged to agricultural cooperatives.[22]

In 1932, Congress passed the Norris-LaGuardia Act which gave certain rights to organized labor. The act prohibited "yellow-dog" contracts, meaning employment contracts that limit a worker's right to join a labor union, gave union members freedom to be undisturbed by employers, and prevented federal courts from halting strikes. A few years later, the government further sanctioned unions and cooperatives, creating democratic work programs through President Franklin Delano Roosevelt's New Deal policies. The Wagner Act of 1935 marked a momentous success for the labor movement under Roosevelt, creating the National Labor Relations Board (NLRB). The Wagner Act gave employees the right to "form and join unions and obligated employers to bargain collectively with unions selected by a majority of the employees in an appropriate bargaining unit."[23] New Deal legislation encouraged the formation of many significant cooperatives, including the Rural Electric Cooperatives, and the financial institutions that supported them.[24]

In a dramatic shift, the 1940s ushered in government policies that actively worked against cooperatives and unions. The German-Soviet Nonaggression Pact of 1939 put anti-socialist and anti-communist pressure on many trade unions. Unions were purged of any left-leaning leaders as a socialist scare gripped the United States. The Taft-Hartley Act of 1947 all but repealed the pro-union Wagner Act, dramatically limiting the power of unions.[25] Taft-Hartley required union officers "to file affidavits affirming that they were not members of the Communist Party or of any organization supporting it."[26] A new type of union emerged— one led by anti-communists and anti-socialists. Taft-Hartley lead to the decline of most cooperatives in the United States (agricultural cooperatives notwithstanding, which were still protected under the Capper-Volstead Act). Ultimately, this harsh political and economic climate made it challenging for cooperatives to survive.

Interest in collectives and cooperatives exploded in the changed political landscape of the 1960s and '70s. The movements that came about—civil rights, women's rights, anti-war—were stimulated by participatory democracy.

The ideals of social harmony and cooperation were no longer associated with Communism. During the '60s and '70s, numerous consumer, media (bookstores, filmmakers), and food cooperatives were formed, although many were "unofficial," and therefore their total number is hard to quantify.[27] Of these unofficial co-ops, John Curl notes:

> These differed from earlier American industrial cooperatives and coop stores mainly in that they chose worker control through the collective consensus decision-making system, rather than the majority-rule managerial systems predominate since the early 19th century. ... They existed under a variety of legal forms. ... Many had no legal existence at all and operated in the fringe areas of the economy. Since capitalist law requires all group "enterprises" to conform to a corporate or partnership structure, the collective structure was often formed into an underground existence.[28]

In the 1980s, the pendulum swung back again. With the onset of the 1980–83 recession and the economic policies of newly elected president Ronald Reagan, including cuts to social programs, tax breaks for corporations, and reduced government regulation, many small businesses, including many newly formed cooperatives, had to shut their doors. Regan's support of corporate consolidation, the weakening of labor unions, and the privatization of public services created a hostile environment for the development of new cooperatives. Many of the consumer cooperatives founded in the 1970s, such as cooperative grocery stores, struggled to remain open.

From the 1990s until the early 2000s, there was little change in the cooperative movement. Nevertheless, a notable moment of progress was marked by the development of regional networks of cooperatives in the Northeast, the Northwest, and the Bay Area. The Network of Bay Area Worker Cooperatives (NoBAWC, pronounced "no boss") was formed in 1994, linking many local worker cooperatives together for mutual aid and support.

The past twenty years have been relatively positive for cooperative businesses. There has been an increase in growth, advocacy, and education within the movement.[29] Much of this is due to the work of the National Cooperative Business Association (NCBA). Originally formed as the Cooperative League in 1916, it supported the formation of the US Federation for Worker Cooperatives (USFWC) in 2004. The USFWC is a membership and advocacy organization, which has laid substantial groundwork for the growth of worker cooperatives in the past two decades. In 2013, it supported the foundation of the Democracy at Work Institute (DAWI), whose mission is education, the promulgation of public resources, and the promotion of workplace democracy. In 2018, the US government passed the Main Street Employee Ownership Act, which provides employee-owned businesses access to Small Business Administration (SBA) loans for the first time in history. The Main Street Act paved the way for the growth of Small Business Development Centers (SBDCs), local agencies that support worker cooperatives through technical assistance and education.[30]

Individual states have also taken action to promote cooperatives. Minnesota adopted their Cooperative Association Act in 2003. Colorado got the ball rolling with a statute for energy cooperatives in 2004, later adopting the Uniform Limited Cooperative Association Act in 2011.[31] California's Worker Cooperative Act went into effect in 2016.[32] In 2022, most states allow for the formation and incorporation of a worker cooperative, however that doesn't mean incorporation is easy.[33]

In a significant ideological shift, cooperatives and unions have recently recognized that they have more to gain from their own intersectionality than they do from mining their ideological differences. In 2009, the United Steelworkers International Union (USW) announced a partnership with Kent State's Ohio Employee-Ownership Center (OEOC) and the Spanish cooperative Mondragón.[34] The Mondragón Cooperative was founded in 1956 by Father José María Arizmendiarrieta to create sustainable and stable jobs for the town of Mondragón, in the Basque region of Spain. It is structured as an umbrella corporation for many smaller cooperatives, serving as an administrative and support structure. In 2022, Mondragón is the largest cooperative in the world. The intent of the USW/OEOC was to bring the Mondragón model of cooperatives to the United States. In 2012, they revealed their hybrid union-co-op model, and in 2017 published the USW *Mondragon Union Co-op Model*, a resource on the formation of union co-ops.[35] United Steelworkers president Leo Gerard explains the model's popularity:

> As the economic crisis festers for many long-term unemployed and underemployed people, the idea of worker-owned and worker-run cooperatives has become ever more appealing as a possible pathway toward an economy that works for everyone. ... [C]ooperatives [provide] a nuts-and-bolts alternative to dominant methods of economic production: they offer an example of a different way of doing business that people can see and experience in their own lives.[36]

The benefits of worker cooperatives are strengthened by a relationship to a union. Workers who elect to not become worker-owners still have a voice through union representation. Unions offer checks and balances for an existing cooperative democracy. Unions also offer their bread-and-butter tools: collective bargaining agreements, grievance procedures, and legal resources to support worker-owned cooperatives' development. Additionally, Rebecca Lurie, founder of the Community and Worker Ownership Project at City University of New York (CUNY) notes, "unions can bring together sector-wide approaches for regulations that raise the floor for wages and benefits and set standards for safe and democratic working conditions across multiple employers."[37] These two worker-forward movements can together combat the ill effects of market-driven competition, in which a small number of employers hold outsized control over the workforce. For context, John Curl writes, "in 1800 there were few wage earners in the US; in 1870 ... over half the workforce consisted of employees; in 1940, about 80 percent; in 2007, 92 percent."[38] Workers need to organize—they already have numbers on their side.

US cooperatives have had a rocky history: peaks with governmental support and ideal economic conditions and declines with pro-free-market legislative and economic policies. This history should be compared with that of other nations to prove that the difficulties co-ops face in the United States are not inevitable but particular to US policy. Unlike in Europe, the United States has no history of socialist parties that support cooperatives or place them within a larger national and ideological context. The most well-known cooperatives, Mondragón in Spain and Emilia Romagna in Italy, are shaped by their own nations' trajectories. Both were founded during periods of government disinvestment which motivated local, ground-up, mutually supportive worker networks, and leveraged past socialist leanings. Cooperatives became a way for businesses and workers to succeed under stressful historic conditions. Today they are integrated into society and enjoy renewed government support.

Mondragón, a town in the Basque region of northern Spain, was economically depressed after the Spanish Civil War. When founded in 1956, the Mondragón Cooperative produced paraffin heaters. From 1970 to 1990—with a strong increase in new cooperatives promoted by Caja Laboral (a workers' credit union), the promotion of cooperative associations and networks, the formation of local groups, and the founding of the Ikerlan Research Centre, a research and development company, in 1974—Mondragón expanded beyond its local region. When Spain was scheduled to join the European Economic Community in 1986, the "Mondragón Co-operative Group," forerunner of the current corporation, was formed. Responding to growing globalization, Mondragón opened production plants in a number of countries, first in Mexico in 1990, and by the end of 2013, in 122 other nations. The goal was to bring component supply closer to cooperative customers' plants, especially in the automotive and domestic appliance sectors. With over 95 cooperatives, 80,000 members, and sales in over 150 countries, Mondragón is the tenth largest business in Spain.[39] The model has proven successful even during economic challenges in part because workers can be relocated to other member co-ops should any one business struggle.

Emilia Romagna is not a co-op, rather it is a region north of Italy surrounding Bologna that is governed by a network of co-ops. The first cooperatives began there in the 1860s, and by the early twentieth century, numerous cooperatives were present in every sector of the economy. In the 1920s, the National Fascist Board of Cooperatives took over all Italian co-ops and removed their autonomy, effectively ending them. Yet Emilia Romagna, a stronghold of Gramscian anarchism, became a center of fascist resistance during World War II. As German military presence in the region was particularly strong, and the disruption of everyday life acutely felt by its citizens, in the absence of the Italian state, local, antifascist, communist partisans stepped in to represent the populace. These partisans formed the only group willing and able to defend the local population, providing them with food and the rule of law. By the end of the war, the Italian Communist Party had an elaborate, entrenched web of local activists, organizers, and community leaders. The cooperative system they initiated would endure from the 1940s to the present day, and form the world's largest and most coherent network of cooperatives. After World War II, the Italian government recognized the value of co-ops as a boon for Italy's particular system of small- and medium-sized businesses, one which allowed for "vertical, horizontal, and complimentary networks through consortia and groupings, supported by financial networks and the strategic role of umbrella organizations."[40] In 2022, cooperatives represent 30 percent of the GDP in the Emilia Romagna region; one of every two residents is a cooperative member, and unemployment remains at the low rate of 4 percent.[41]

Both Mondragón and Emilia Romagna have roots specific to their unique cultural and political circumstance. However, their longevity over a changing economic and political landscape, their integration into national policy, and Mondragón's expanding reach, proves the sustainability of the model beyond their own regions. By contrast, the lack of sustained government support of the cooperative model in the United States has led to confusing legislation, and the absence of general education regarding co-ops and their benefits. Despite these challenges, cooperatives have nevertheless persevered, and in recent years enjoyed accelerated growth. More and more, we understand their advantages. Cooperatives and democratic workplaces improve the lives of workers. Cooperative workers build equity and wealth through ownership, minority voices are uplifted, and workers are more engaged in their work.[42] Cooperatives often establish a wage differential, commonly 3:1, meaning that the top earner makes no more than three times the lowest paid worker.[43] This stands in stark contrast with traditional, publicly traded companies, wherein CEOs can make up to 351 times the salary of their lowest paid worker.[44] Democratic workplaces are typically transparent about wages, and during economic turmoil, owners can collectively lower pay or democratically decide to use reserves to support a few months' of lower income.[45] Because of their democratic nature, cooperatives uplift minority voices and are inherently feminist. More women and BIPOC workers benefit from ownership and wealth accumulation in cooperatives as opposed to traditional workplaces.[46] In an industry like architecture—in which women and BIPOC architects represent 37 percent and 32 percent respectively of all architecture staff, yet only 21 percent and 14 percent respectively of principals and partners—collective structural help is needed.[47] Worker participation in an organization can "reduce management abuse, increase workers' skills and autonomy and cultivate a greater sense of pride in one's work."[48] Through worker-ownership, exploitative labor practices diminish, and worker engagement rises.

While architecture firms could take advantage of all these benefits, the model has yet to proliferate in white collar industries, where professionals have ignored a movement supposedly aimed at business production and distribution. This class-based stratification of cooperatives has closed the doors, culturally and financially, to the idea of joint ownership. A glimpse into the professionalization of architecture demonstrates why this gap seems so difficult to bridge.

Chapter 2:
A Brief Synopsis of Architecture

There are many great scholars who have written about the origins of architecture and architects throughout history. A few are referenced here, but this too-brief synopsis is meant only to give context for the profession's approach to its workers and those workers' potential to organize as cooperatives.

Historically, the term *architect*—from the Greek *architekton*—referred to a multitude of practitioners including artists, temple designers, and ship builders. Even former slaves of the Roman Empire became architects.[49] The Roman author and military architect Vitruvius, however, argued that architecture was a distinguished and learned career. In fifteenth-century Italy, figures like Filippo Brunelleschi, Donato Bramante, and Michelangelo were called "architects" because they were not builders but rather the producers or creators of building designs. Professions, in the form we understand them today, arose in the mid-eighteenth century when wealthy English gentlemen studied to become experts in a given field of knowledge, including architecture.

The emergence of architecture as a profession in the United States evolved more slowly. Separation from the building trades and creation of the architecture education system, took more time to develop in the United States than in Europe. In the eighteenth century, during peak colonial development, the architect was not yet formally distinguished from the builder or the craftsman.[50] Master craftsmen, also known as "building mechanics," had provided design and construction services on US soil since the founding of early European colonies in the seventeenth century. If these craftsmen also drafted plans and supervised construction, they were called architects.[51] European architects like Henri Latrobe, who had worked in a professional architectural office in England, were surprised by the lack of established practice in the United States and initially clashed with the master craftsmen of the time.[52]

Toward the second half of the eighteenth century, a handful of the American elite, including Peter Harrison, Thomas Jefferson, William Thorton, and Charles Bulfinch, viewed the act of design as a hobby. They all required master craftsmen to build their designs. These gentlemen were not pursuing the practice of architecture as a means of income; they viewed it as a cultural pastime or the practice of self-expression.[53]

The development of private practices with divisions of labor, professional societies, and the first architectural schools began in the nineteenth century. Sociologist David Brain describes the shifting state of the profession:

Between 1820 and 1840 there was a qualitative change in the occupational roles underlying the production of architecture in the United States. During this period, it became common to engage an architect specifically as a designer, at least for public buildings, churches, and fashionable houses. ... The work of producing drawings providing architects with the practical foundation for a discipline of design, and its anchoring point in the division of labor.[54]

This era of the draftsman-architect initiated the separation of architects from the building trades. Westward expansion and the Industrial Revolution created a boom in the speculative real estate market, requiring more building designs to be produced. The act of drafting was driven by the desire for increasingly complicated and stylized buildings as a result of speculation.[55] The draftsman-architect could learn his trade from studying, as an apprentice, under other draftsman-architects rather than craftsmen/builders; this effectively created a career path outside of the building trades. Thus was born the architectural practice, structured under the master-apprentice model.

In the eighteenth century, the profession was led by an exclusive class of aristocratic men who, reliant on social status and familial connections, were able to pursue an education in Europe since the United States had not yet established an architecture school of its own.[56] This education provided familiarity with the various emerging styles in Europe desirable to clients driving the speculative building boom in the United States; an education in "style" provided the means to success in the emerging profession.

The development of blueprint technology in 1842 meant that fewer draftsmen were needed for drawing production. This newly competitive environment benefited those who were formally educated over those who were not.[57] There were very few opportunities for the less-than-wealthy to receive an architectural education that provided upward mobility, moving an aspiring candidate beyond being a draftsman. This maintained architecture as a profession for the wealthy.[58] Although the language of "master" and "apprentice" remained in architecture for decades longer, we can understand the division of labor within the field in the mid-eighteenth century as bosses employing draftsmen.[59] Architecture was evolving from a hobby or a gentlemanly pursuit into a business.

The Move Toward Professionalization: The Establishment of the AIA
It is estimated that in 1840 there were only six architects working in New York City; by 1860 there were 600, many of them immigrants from England and Germany.[60] US architects believed that the expanding field threatened their position in society and the public's perception of architecture, diluting their value. In addition, there was still overlap between the building trades and the practice of architecture, confusing its domain. To combat these factors and control the growth of the profession, architects organized in 1857 to found the American Institute of Architects (AIA). Their goal was to create a distinction between educated and competent professionals and the uneducated, gatekeeping through the apparatus of membership.[61]

In the 1860s, following the US Civil War, cities underwent massive expansion due to immigration, the emergence of mass transit systems, and the development

of new building materials. Simultaneously, the creation of building codes meant 19
that cities developed bureaucracies to "guarantee competence and technical
expertise" for their growth.[62] To maintain the flow of incoming work, architects
needed to professionalize in order to meet the needs and technical requirements
of growing cities.[63] While the AIA had mostly shuttered during the war, postwar
reinvigoration spawned a new type of architect: the professional. Membership in
the AIA remained exclusive and fraternal; members represented a group of men
with similar ideas about the profession. The exclusivity of membership enhanced
the caché of a "professionalized" office.

Not long after this building boom, the first architectural school in the United
States was founded at the Massachusetts Institute of Technology (MIT) in 1868.
The first four architectural schools in the United States—MIT, Cornell University, Illinois Institute of Technology, and Syracuse University—were under the
direction of AIA members.[64] Indeed, the development of a professional education
was a key tenet of the AIA. Architects of the time "looked down their noses with
pity for the great unwashed public."[65] The AIA's Committee on Education saw
itself as representing a "body of gentlemen scholars, not just a body of men in the
business of architecture."[66] Through education, the AIA, concerned with perpet-
uating the elite status of architecture as a "learned profession," could distinguish
educated scholars from uneducated businessmen and builders. Their authority was not in question as the prominence of the organization had already been
established decades prior.

Deepening Regulation and Emerging Corporate Rule
The next step in architecture's professionalization was the establishment of a system of licensure. For several years, architects outside of AIA lobbied their state
legislators to create a system of licensure which would protect the public from
builders' incompetence and further distinguish the educated from the uneducated. The collapse of buildings erected by uneducated practitioners is cited as
a main driver behind the push for licensure, but one can't ignore the self-interested hegemony of white, wealthy men at this time in history. Several times these
bills were denied due either to legislative backlog or because they were thought
to unfairly limit competition.[67] In 1897, Illinois became the first state to require
licensure, just a few years after instituting one of the nation's first building codes.
California followed suit in 1902.[68] In 1897, it was estimated that AIA members
constituted less than 20 percent of all practicing architects.[69] Licensure, in the
early states that adopted it, acted as a tool for legitimization for architects looking
to distinguish themselves from the less "competent."

Regardless of the benefit it provided, the prospect of licensure caused turmoil within the AIA. Members could not agree on the relationship of licensure
to membership in the organization. By the time consensus was achieved, state
licensure had already taken hold. The AIA's position was that the institute itself
provided a superior licensure system:

> We do not condemn the state licensing system, we simply assert that it is an indif-
> ferent substitute for a more competent licensing power that at present has insuf-
> ficient recognition—the Institute itself.[70]

The AIA suggested that as an organization they held more expertise to determine competency than the emerging state-regulated system. Membership in the AIA implied competence and professionalism above and beyond state law. The organization eventually changed its position once it was clear that state licensure was not going away, as more states adopted licensure statutes. Having accepted licensure, AIA membership was only available to licensed architects or to those on a licensure path.[71]

In the first decades of the twentieth century, AIA membership remained relatively low due to the significant barriers to entry that the organization had put into place. In 1930, only thirty-two states had licensure registration laws, leaving government agencies to rely on AIA membership for an architect's proof of competency. Membership in the AIA surged during the New Deal, which created several programs for unemployed and underemployed architects, reaching over 4,000 members by 1935.[72] The New Deal created the Public Works Administration (PWA) which during its tenure from 1933 to 1943 injected immense fiscal stimulus into the building industry. By 1939, it had contributed $3.8 billion toward roughly 34,000 projects. Additionally, the Historic American Building Survey (HABS) hired one thousand previously unemployed architects to document "America's antique buildings".[73] Another noteworthy program was the Tennessee Valley Association (TVA) which created large scale infrastructure operated under democratic governance.[74] The AIA supported these programs, and many of the architects hired were AIA members.

Pro-Corporate America

The professional status of architecture has mostly exempted architects from competition. Engineering and architecture, like medicine and law, were exempt from antitrust legislation under the Sherman Act.[75] This remained the status quo until the 1970s, when professions were subject to antitrust lawsuits for the first time. This was largely due to the pro-corporate policies of the Nixon and Reagan administrations.[76] Lawsuits targeted minimum fee schedules typically included in the ethical standards (e.g., codes of ethics) of professional organizations. These fee schedules were considered a form of non-competitive price-fixing.[77] Over and over again, throughout the 1970s and '80s, many professions, including architecture, were brought to court on the grounds of antitrust legislation.

In 1972, in one of the first cases against the profession of architecture, the AIA and the Department of Justice (DOJ) entered into a consent decree that prohibited fee setting and required the AIA to send all members a copy of the decree and an annual report for the next five years, demonstrating steps toward compliance.[78] A similar ruling (and a failed attempt to overturn it) by the National Society of Professional Engineers (NSPE) demonstrated the tightening grip of the DOJ on professions.[79] In 1975, a private lawsuit targeted a component of the code of ethics, namely "supplanting"—or stealing another architect's client. The court ruled that supplanting suppressed competition and was therefore illegal.[80] In 1990, a second consent decree was signed between the AIA and the DOJ stating, "nothing shall prohibit any individual architect or architectural firm, acting alone, from expressing an opinion about architectural prices or competition."[81] These agreements weakened the AIA's power as a professional organization.

The message was clear: there shall be no participation in any activity that could be construed as collusion.

Up until this point in time, the AIA had maintained a stronghold over the profession, directing its development and protecting it from the law in some fashion. DOJ legal actions reduced the perceived power of the AIA, as the organization was no longer able to protect architects from antitrust legislation. With weakened support, firms had to fend for themselves. Intra-firm efficiencies became crucial to maintain the lowest possible fees, sparking a new race to the bottom. With this focus on efficiency, office management practice began to consume firm structure, and strict managerial hierarchies—the Taylorization of architecture—became the standard in large firms.[82]

The Past Thirty Years

The past thirty years have witnessed the triumph of the large architecture firm. Large offices are able to take advantage of their scale: lower overhead costs per employee, in-house Human Resources and Information Technology departments, better purchasing power, and in-house expertise; all efficiencies resulting from the division of labor and strict managerial hierarchies. As a consequence, the number of large firms with fifty-plus employees has increased. The share of firms with fifty or more employees grew from 3 percent in 1996 to 5 percent in 1999, nearly doubling.[83] The share of firms with over fifty employees in 2022 represents 6.3 percent of all firms. Notably, more than half of all architectural workers are employed at firms with over fifty employees.[84] Small firms, on the other hand, suffer disproportionally. Not only do they lack the above advantages, they have less institutional knowledge to determine an intuited "consensus" for "standard" fees.[85] In 1999, small firms represented 76 percent of all firms but held only 17 percent of all billings. In 2019, the percentage of small firms represented 75.2 percent of all firms yet held only 12.8 percent of all billings.[86] Over the past twenty years, the same percentage of small firms are fighting over a decreasing share of industry billings. Small architecture firms are struggling to survive on very thin margins. As a result, small firms—which, numerically, are the backbone of the profession—have responded by adopting ad hoc organizational strategies to stay afloat in the harsh economic climate.

The AIA has documented changes in the profession using their Firm Survey Report since 1979.[87] The organization's business model, selling sample contracts and collecting membership dues, supports firm owners rather than employees. They provide testing resources and "networking opportunities" for employees but have yet to address labor malpractice in the profession.[88] Membership benefits include access to sample contracts, MasterSpec access (a resource for product specifications), shipping discounts at FedEx and rental car discounts at Hertz, and access to legal information, all of which are aimed to support business owners. Of course, firms with a greater number of employees deliver greater dues to the AIA, and the organization therefore takes special interest in larger offices.

Despite the member-only (read: incomplete) framing of the profession offered by the AIA, and its explicit disregard for firm employees, architecture as a practice intrinsically fits the cooperative model. The production of architecture is reliant on many different actors with different skills that must cooperate to complete a given project. Projects flow in a nonlinear manner that defies Taylorization. In this era of information technology, shared/open information, and knowledge work, architecture is ripe for cooperativization. A French study shows that knowledge-intensive industries, such as architecture, are particularly successful—in terms of productivity, minimizing inequality, and profit—when organized democratically.[89]

The previous two chapters have laid out the trajectories of co-ops and the profession of architecture with the aim of showing their historical mistrust of one another. The next chapter highlights moments of actual, possible, and commonly overlooked intersections between architecture and labor-forward, cooperative models of business.

Chapter 3:
Where and How the Intersections
Became Possible

The profession of architecture has maintained a hands-off relationship with the labor movement, a political detachment supported by the AIA. The word "worker" does not exist in their documents, and employees are identified as "rising professionals." As the overall economic climate in the United States has become more "entrepreneurial" over the last thirty years (read: free-market, anti-labor), the relationship between architecture and worker-supported business structures has grown ever thinner. Firms maximize efficiencies to eke out maximum profits at the expense of their staff. It is therefore necessary for architects to be reminded of other organizational possibilities.

Precedents

In the 1920s, architects experimented with new business models. In cities like Los Angeles and Washington, DC, there are cases where up to fifty individual architects incorporated as a single stock corporation to bid on public projects as a group.[90] These groups—the first examples of US architectural cooperatives—understood that they were more likely to get work as a collective of architects rather than as individual offices. Following cooperative principles, members of these firms received one vote in matters of the corporation, no matter the number of shares they held. Profits and losses were distributed to all partners, and sometimes directed toward future projects. Some of these collective organizations even provided design services for the AIA. However, not long after this entity type emerged, the AIA outlawed the practice of collectivization.[91] State law in some jurisdictions further reinforced this position: because registration was tied to an individual, architectural "service could not wholly be performed by a corporation."[92] Architectural services were tied to an individual's name and a single license, rather than to the business entity. This determination by the AIA reinforced the individual nature of licensure and hence of the profession, denying the opportunity for collaborations between multiple licensed architects.

During the 1930s, architects formed another type of collaborative organization operating with democratic principles, this time sponsored by the federal government through policies enacted under the New Deal. From 1934 to 1937, twenty select architects were pulled from their private practices and relocated to Washington, DC, as members of the Office of the Supervising Architect.[93] This program, and its architects, directed and designed many of the federal projects built during this period. Eventually, however, these architects returned to their individual private practices.[94]

One of the first intersections between the profession of architecture and the labor movement occurred in 1920. Union leaders were considering draftsmen and office workers as potential tradesmen to organize. In response, the Board of the AIA argued that the profession of architecture was not subject to the same regulations as industrial trades and issued the following decree:

> [T]he profession must continue to develop along professional lines rather than commercial or industrial lines; that architecture and the welfare of those engaged in its practice cannot be advanced by machine-shop methods; that the chapters should encourage societies of draftsmen who would regard their calling as a profession and not a trade.[95]

By 1920, AIA membership included all registered architects who hired draftsmen to staff their offices. If draftsmen were unionized, their labor would be more expensive, they would require benefits, and they would enjoy collective bargaining rights. By considering the act of drafting a "profession" rather than a trade, architect-employers were able to skirt the risk of unionization, further stratifying architects above the working class.

In 1933, the National Industrial Recovery Act (NIRA) required industries to establish regulating codes, including wage standards. The AIA responded by setting wages with the stipulation that "architectural employees having had at least two years' office experience as draftsmen or its equivalent ... be paid not less than 50 cents an hour," just 10 cents more than the lowest category of pay to general workers.[96] The incredibly low wage angered draftsmen, who had just been distinguished as "professionals" by the AIA to avoid their potential unionization.[97] These draftsmen organized with other workers effected by high unemployment and low wages to form the Federation of Architects, Engineers, Chemists and Technicians (FAECT).[98] FAECT successfully opposed this proposed minimum wage in Washington, DC, at public wage code hearings.[99]

FAECT went on to act as a de facto trade union and activist organization supporting professional workers, which the AIA was unwilling to do. They affiliated themselves with the Congress of Industrial Organizations (CIO) in 1937.[100] The Federation mobilized around certain policies of the New Deal, critiquing their efficacy and ultimately arguing that those policies had not done enough to address the quality of housing and the negative effects of urban development.[101] The organization made New Deal policies better for both architectural professionals and the public they served.[102]

As an organization, FAECT would not last. The German-Soviet Nonaggression Pact aggravated anti-socialist and anti-communist sentiment in the United States toward all unions, including FAECT. Representative Martin Dies, chairman of the House Special Committee on Un-American Activities, charged that the "union as a whole is under the complete domination of the Communist Party."[103] There was sustained pressure on the CIO to separate itself from supposed communist influence. In March 1946, in a strategic move to evade anti-communist pressure, FAECT merged with Local 231 of the United Office and Professional

Workers of America (UOPWA). Yet the strategy failed, and in 1950 FAECT was ejected from the CIO entirely due to its "communist influence."[104] FAECT ultimately collapsed, like many other unions at that time, an indication of the government's fear of workers' strength.

In the 1950s, the AIA again rejected a possible relationship with the labor movement. At the time, Kohler plumbing factory workers were striking with support from the United Auto Workers union. The striking workers sent letters to architects asking them to stop specifying Kohler products due to poor labor conditions in factories. Alerted to the letters, the AIA met with labor leaders and convinced them to stop the letter campaign and took no further action to support Kohler workers.[105] This position, one of complete dismissal of responsibility and the power of solidarity, further entrenched architects as professional set apart from the "working" class.

The AIA did not shift its policies in the 1960s and '70s, but general sentiment did. These two decades were witness to many anti-capitalist collective and collaborative actions in numerous disciplines, including architecture. In 1965, the Prickly Mountain collective formed in Vermont when a group of disenchanted architecture students from the Yale School of Architecture went there to build instead of read. As pioneers of the design/build movement—which contended that designers shouldn't be drawing blueprints if they don't know anything about construction—founders David Sellers and Jim Statton built a number of iconic houses that have since gained local notoriety. Similarly, Ant Farm was progressive regarding their ideas on collectives and the role of architecture in society. One of Ant Farm's founders, Doug Michels, described their motivations: "We wanted to be an architecture group that was more like a rock band." As Michels put it, "the founding of the name was indicative of how Ant Farm worked: the right idea comes, everybody acknowledges it is the right idea and instantly adopts it."[106] In the same spirit, Paolo Soleri's Arcosanti left civilization to escape to the remote high desert of Arizona with the intent to build their own self-sufficient settlement.

Simultaneously, similar movements were happening outside the United States. In Chile, several architectural collaboratives formed between the 1950s and '60s as a direct result of the teachings of Hungarian immigrant Tibor Weiner—namely Schapira Eskenazi Architecture (SEA) and Taller de Arquitectura y Urbanismo (TAU)—whose members went on to found the Art, Urban Planning, Construction, and Architecture Cooperative (AUCA), where they published a journal featuring their ideas on collaborative social architecture.[107] The UK's Archigram was founded in the early 1960s,[108] along with several Italian collaboratives: Archizoom, Superstudio,[109] Gruppo 9999, and Gruppo Strum.[110]

One of the earliest and best-known architectural collaboratives in the United States is The Architect's Collaborative (TAC), a firm adhering to the values of democracy, collaboration, and modernism.[111] TAC operated as an unincorporated architectural cooperative upon its inception in 1945. Founding members had a say in the governance and direction of the office, and designs were handled collaboratively. As they grew—eventually becoming the largest architectural practice in the US by number of employees in the 1960s—they gradually departed from this way of working, juggling the distinction between a collaboration of equals and a partnership between founding members and employees. TAC officially incorporated in 1963, solidifying stratification between owners and employees. The practice struggled to maintain its original identity under the pressure of its own rapid growth and general capitalist forces acting on the profession. With systemic conflict weighing on the founding members of TAC, the firm collapsed in 1995.[112]

The forces of political economy that increasingly supported growth and corporatism in the 1970s took their toll on worker-forward, collaborative efforts in architecture. The same neoliberal forces identified with Reaganomics that promoted competition and economic maximization left almost no examples of collaboration beyond the ongoing efforts of TAC. Current reaction to the negative outcomes spawned by neoliberalism, in society in general and in architecture in particular, is now inspiring change. It has become clear that architecture firms, small firms in particular, must not treat other firms as the competition (i.e., the enemy), but collaborate for the sake of an empowered profession against the real culprit harming their interests: the short-term trajectories of private development.

The Present and Future: The Case for the Architectural Cooperative

While there are several design firms in the process of incorporation as cooperatives, at the time of this publication there are twelve incorporated architecture and design cooperatives in the United States:

1. South Mountain Company, founded in 1975, is a beneficial corporation located in West Tisbury, Martha's Vineyard, Massachusetts.
2. Warrenstreet Architects, founded in 1990, is a stock corporation located in Concord, New Hampshire.
3. Design Cooperative (DCOOP), founded in 2007, is an LLC in Jacksonville, Florida.
4. Co-op Architecture (a fictitious business name, or DBA, for Collaborative Operandi Architecture) is an LLC, founded in 2011 in Aberdeen, South Dakota.
5. Third Place Design Cooperative, founded in 2014, is a Washington Cooperative Association in Seattle, Washington.
6. Oxbow Design Build, founded in 2015 and organized as an employee cooperative in 2019, is located in East Hampton, Massachusetts.
7. Uxo architects, founded in 2016 and cooperativized in 2018, is a stock corporation in Los Angeles, California.
8. Root Volume Landscape architects, founded in 2017, is a nonprofit in Oakland, California.
9. CoEverything, founded in 2018, is an LLC in Dorchester, Massachusetts.
10. CivicStudio founded in 2019 is an LLC in New Orleans, Louisiana.
11. Design Anarchy Cooperative incorporated in 2022 as a cooperative corporation in Colorado, while operating in Indianapolis, Indiana.
12. Placetailor is a developer-architecture cooperative, incorporated as an LLC in 2021 in Roxbury, Massachusetts.

Various incorporation strategies, ranging from a nonprofit to an LLC to an employee cooperative, are used by these offices. Ranging in size from two to over forty people, each has its own internal operating and management strategy, meaning that some offices choose to stratify into a hierarchy, similar to a traditional office, while others operate more horizontally.

It is inspiring to see these offices embrace the cooperative model. However, a mere twelve cooperative offices of the estimated 67,000 architecture firms in the United States is barely noteworthy.[113]

Other Cooperatives

While worker co-ops are rare, several are currently in the process of incorporating as such. There is more and more interest in network cooperatives wherein multiple firms, not necessarily worker-owned, take advantage of shared knowledge and power in lieu of competing against one another.[114] These network memberships types include the purchasing cooperative, the marketing cooperative, the cooperative conglomerate, and of course, the union-cooperative.

A purchasing cooperative creates purchasing power through increased member numbers that reduce direct costs to individual firms. By having a larger staff, large architecture offices are able to access the benefits of reduced rates through the network-wide, shared, high employee count. This is true for health care plans, software subscriptions, professional services, and even equipment purchases. A purchasing cooperative provides these benefits to smaller offices, ultimately lowering overhead costs for member firms. On a local scale, this might translate into a cooperative co-working space with shared Wi-Fi, printers, and a shop.

A marketing cooperative is a type of producer cooperative common in the agriculture industry, where many individual farmers sell their products to a single cooperative with a large market share. This is reproduceable in architecture. Small offices can join together to market themselves together using a referral cooperative. A client contacts the cooperative because of aligned values, product recognition, etc., and the co-op either refers the client to a particular firm or individual within the network best suited to the project or provides architectural services itself directly. When enacted on a national scale, the referral co-op model creates potential challenges due to varying licensure and Practice Act requirements in each state.

The cooperative conglomerate is a holding company for several small cooperatives. A portion of profit from individual co-ops go to the conglomerate and is then redistributed to each member cooperative proportionally as defined by its bylaws. This helps less profitable firms become more profitable by redistributing wealth between affiliated businesses. The cooperative conglomerate can operate nationally and own businesses in many states, which allows member firms to maintain their local market share while benefitting from geographic diversity.

A multi-stakeholder or hybrid cooperative is one with multiple classes of owners. This can be any combination of consumers, producers, and workers, including volunteer members. Different member classes might have equal voting power, or they might not. For example, if an architecture firm wants to share office space but not participate in a marketing cooperative, a multi-stakeholder cooperative would be applicable.

A platform cooperative is a cooperatively owned and operated business that runs a digital platform like an app or website. These apps are designed to directly benefit workers rather than funnel profits to shareholders. Examples include the Drivers Cooperative, a driver-owned rideshare service; and Fairbnb, which gives 50 percent of its revenue to a local community project. In the field of architecture, a platform cooperative creates a resource on which to share software, communicate, and potentially support a labor trade system.[115]

The union cooperative model could be very beneficial for the profession, representing firms of all sizes. In addition to supporting the formation of worker cooperatives, the union would support all architectural workers, cooperativized or not, with bargaining rights and legal aid. The state of the profession in 2022 requires a "both/and" approach. Unions would help architectural workers win much-needed battles regarding wages, hours, and employer accountability.

Any of these network models would drastically alter the current self-contained nature of small architecture offices, whose success relies on self-sufficiency. By offering administrative services and purchasing power, these networks would free up capital for higher wages and better equipment. Resources could be shared among multiple offices, including a standardized contract that would ensure a democratic joint venture between offices in order to undertake larger projects together. Firms could join together to purchase insurance, or software licenses, at a discounted rate.[116] A bookkeeper and a CPA could be hired by the cooperative to support all offices within its network. With extra capital and potential labor sharing between firms, offices could be free from the burden of taking on too many projects at once just to pay the bills. ArchiTeam, an Australian nonprofit cooperative network, is already proving the benefits of the model. With over 900 member firms, they are able to provide insurance, contracts and marketing for their members at a discounted rate.[117]

In closing, a note on Employee Stock Ownership Plans (ESOPs). ESOPs have garnered a lot attention recently and in the name of "employee ownership." This model, which creates a system for profit sharing among employees, is not a cooperative. It is often selected by larger corporations, consisting of 100 employees or more, because of its tax and name-recognition benefits, namely the label "employee-owned." The ESOP model does not require any level of democratic governance or transparency from participating employers, and the claim of "ownership" seems more of a marketing ploy for future employees than a real benefit for current ones.[118] Nonetheless, profit sharing among workers is certainly better than nothing.

All architects, even those not motivated by the cooperative ethos, need to understand the most practical and self-interested aspect of the business: succession planning. The AIA finds that 88 percent of firms with over 50 employees have plans in place, while only 9 percent of small firms do, defined as firms with fewer than 10 employees. In total, 76 percent of firms do not have a succession plan in place.[119] The baby boomer generation controls over twelve million privately-owned businesses, valuing roughly $10 trillion.[120] Over the next ten to fifteen years, this generation will be retiring and looking to sell their businesses, a market trend known as the Silver Tsunami. Corporate consolidation poses a threat not only to the livelihood of workers, but also to a company's prosperity.[121] ESOPs are a popular path for setting up the conditions needed for smooth succession planning. But planners should consider going beyond that, including selling the business to their employees. Keeping their business in the hands of their employees assumes continuity of service to the established community and provides employees with a new opportunity to build equity.[122]

The hope is that those attentive to practical business considerations also realize that there is a fundamental, ethical component inherent in cooperatives. The trust they require and inspire, the belief that group success is more important than individual success, represent an ethical way of doing business. No one should ever enter into a cooperative for selfish, profit-driven reasons. Worker cooperatives are a component of a much larger movement in solidarity with a just and equitable economy.[123] This movement utilizes cooperatives as a way to take back control of human labor from employers and harness it, through the workings of a democratic process. These movements need architects. Whether it's the development of community land trusts or providing knowledge of the permitting process at a community meeting, architectural knowledge is incredibly valuable to society at large.

practice practice

Part II
Cooperative Legal Entity Types and Tax Code

Part 1 laid out the conceptual and historical argument in support of architectural cooperatives. Part 2 offers practical advice for forming a worker-cooperative business. It reviews complicated business protocols and legal frameworks supporting cooperativization, particularly in a profession like architecture.

While applicable network cooperative models have already been described, this section focuses on the single-worker cooperative entity. As I argued in chapter 3, architecture, like many design professions, naturally lends itself to the cooperative model given that a complex web of actors and tasks are required for project delivery. Beyond accepting the advantages of cooperation over competition and/or disruptive hierarchies, ownership of one's labor and its products need not be a distant dream. Young or small firms and their architectural workers can be owners from the start.

As outlined in part 1, the US capitalist economy is geared toward competition, not cooperation. It follows that cooperative business are not foregrounded in our business and tax structure, and therefore must adapt to one of a multitude of configurations—legal entities, tax regimes, and values—which are described below. Note that Employee Stock Ownership Plans (ESOPs) do not provide actual worker-ownership and will only be mentioned cursorily. The end of part 2 provides an assessment of alternative cooperative configurations beyond the single business and explores ideas of activism meant to make forming cooperatives in the field of architecture easier to accomplish.

Aside from legal and tax frameworks, there are an internationally recognized set of principles, namely the Rochdale Principles,[124] that guide cooperatives:

- **Voluntary and Open Membership**
  Cooperatives are voluntary organizations, open to all persons able to use their services and willing to accept the responsibilities of membership, without gender, social, racial, political, or religious discrimination.

· **Democratic Member Control**
Cooperatives are democratic organizations controlled by their members, and members actively participate in setting policies and making decisions. People serve as elected representatives and are accountable to their members. In primary cooperatives, members have equal voting rights: one member, one vote.

· **Member Economic Participation**
Members contribute equitably to, and democratically control, the capital of their cooperative. At least part of that capital is the common property of the cooperative. Members usually receive limited compensation, if any, on capital invested as a condition of membership. Members allocate surpluses for any and all of the following purposes: developing their cooperative; setting up reserves, part of which would be indivisible; benefiting members in proportion to their work for the cooperative; and supporting other activities approved by the membership.

· **Autonomy and Independence**
Cooperatives are autonomous, self-help organizations controlled by their members. If they enter into agreements with other organizations, including governments, or raise capital from external sources, they do so on terms that ensure democratic control by their members and maintain their cooperative autonomy.

· **Education, Training, and Information**
Cooperatives provide education and training for their members, elected representatives, managers, and employees so that they can contribute effectively to the development of their cooperative. Cooperatives inform the general public, particularly young people and opinion leaders, about the nature and benefits of cooperation.

· **Cooperation among Cooperatives**
Cooperatives serve their members most effectively, and strengthen the cooperative moment, by working together through local, national, regional, and international structures and institutions.

· **Concern for Community**
Cooperatives work for the sustainable development of their communities through policies approved by their members.

It is important to emphasize that cooperatives are not for everyone, and they should not be forced onto an organization that does not truly believe in its principles. While politically organized as a democracy, most US citizens' experience with democratic practice is limited to casting a ballot once every four years; socially and economically our organizations do not function democratically, especially not our places of work. Learning these practices takes time, and there is often initial resistance to some fundamental values of cooperatives. In a culture focused on maximum profits, it's hard to justify the additional organizational expense to train and teach democratic governance. Nevertheless, cooperative efficiency can be learned, and democratic workplaces (full cooperatives or no) have proven to be incredibly successful.[125]

The International Cooperative Alliance (ICA) officially defines worker cooperatives as "an autonomous association of persons united voluntarily to meet their common economic, social, and cultural needs and aspirations through a jointly-owned and democratically-controlled enterprise."[126] However, there are several ways that we can define a cooperative—technically, legally, and in practice.

Worker cooperatives differ from traditional businesses in three ways. First, workers are owners of the business entity; they have an ownership stake. Not all workers must become owners, but there needs to be an open path for any worker to become a co-owner of the organization. Traditional businesses, by contrast, guard ownership closely. Second, when a business entity is established, shares must be distributed to the owners (the number of shares distributed and the total number of shares varies from business to business). Worker cooperatives require that workers democratically control the enterprise, meaning that one worker-owner gets one vote regardless of the number of shares held (see fig. 1). Typical corporations, by contrast, use weighted voting and profit distribution based on the percentage equity held by an investor, thus creating a power imbalance between owners (see fig. 2). Third, worker cooperatives require the democratic distribution of earnings, rather than distributing profits proportionally to the number of shares held (see fig. 3). None of these practices mean that all workers must have

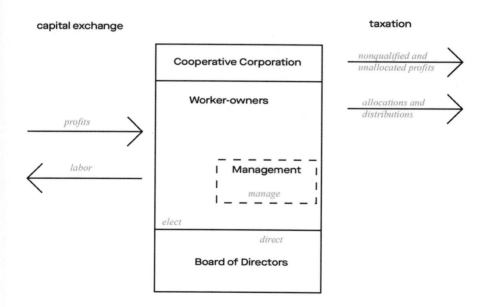

In worker-owner cooperatives, the workers' labor and subsequent profits are shared among worker-owners. Worker-owners elect the board of directors who direct the firm—one worker, one vote.

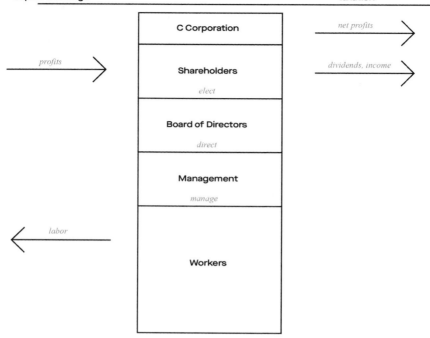

In traditional corporations, profits created from workers' labor is shared only with those who have an ownership stake in the firm. Workers are managed from the top down, and have no say in firm governance or finance.

the same salary; salaries can vary based on experience, similar to the operation of traditional businesses, and internal hierarchies between workers can remain in place. Cooperatives do not require a horizontal structure. However, varied distributions of salary and hierarchy are transparent and agreed upon by all.

The term "cooperative" can refer to a specific entity type (legally defined), an internal way of structuring a business, or a method of taxation.[127] This multitude of definitions can be especially challenging for architects to grasp, given that the professional title "architect" is delegated by the state and applies only to those with licensure. Most states have a cooperative statute available for the formation of worker cooperatives, but to navigate that statue is quite complex. There might be other reasons not to choose a cooperative corporation statute as a route to incorporation, and businesses might opt for a legal workaround instead. Businesses can choose the entity type that best suits their needs, and tailor their internal structure and operations through bylaws or other governing organizational documents to function like a cooperative.

The following is a general overview of the concepts and components of cooperative entities; it does not take the place of professional legal advice.

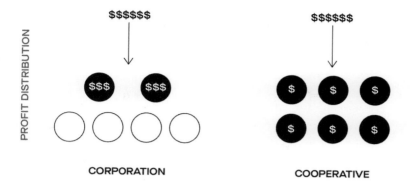

Unlike traditional corporations, cooperatives distribute money among all worker-owners. Workers directly benefit from their own labor. Shared distributions allow for more people to build equity over time than in a traditional corporation.

ENTITY TYPE

Bylaws and Articles of Incorporation

There are many available incorporation types: sole proprietorships, partnerships, corporations, LLCs, LLPs, and nonprofits. Of these types, a few are better suited for cooperatives. Most cooperatives are incorporated as Limited Liability Corporations (LLCs) or Cooperative Corporations, which are a distinct entity type available in some states.[128] There are many factors involved in deciding what entity type an organization will choose. A common deciding factor is how owners are classified with regards to employment law. In corporations, workers are considered employees and therefore require minimum wages, payroll tax deductions, workers' compensation, and other regulations adjudicating employment.[129] In an LLC, however, owners are not considered employees and do not receive wages, but rather draw on the company's account. This distinction is particularly valuable to businesses that do not immediately turn a profit and need flexibility regarding wages and payroll taxes.

Nearly every state has an agricultural cooperative statute, and most states have a cooperative statute that could facilitate the formation of worker cooperatives. Each state limits the purpose of the cooperative and regulates what types of businesses qualify as a worker cooperative.[130] This means that the terrain is quite complex, and templates of incorporation (such as standardized articles of incorporation or bylaws) need to be reviewed by legal counsel before incorporation can be complete. This is a huge deterrent for small organizations that have little start-up capital available to hire an attorney prior to incorporation.

A few states have adopted the Uniform Limited Cooperative Association Act, meant to combine the benefits of the LLC model and the cooperative model and aimed at bringing outside capital into cooperatives. The act is designed to be adopted by states using uniform state laws.[131] However, there is tension in the cooperative community regarding this model because of the association of outside investment. Many believe that a cooperative's prosperity should come from the labor of workers alone, while others see the need for outside investment to support business. In 2022, only eight states have adopted the act: Kentucky, Utah, Vermont, District of Columbia, Oklahoma, Nebraska, Washington, and Colorado.[132]

Incorporation across state lines is also possible. Many businesses choose to incorporate LLCs in Delaware, for example, for its cheaper incorporation fees and taxes. Colorado could be considered "the Delaware of cooperative law," as it has a plethora of cooperative statues available for use by diverse industries.[133] However, a big reason to incorporate in the state where a business is located is to control in what jurisdictions the business might be sued. A business can be sued in its state of incorporation *and* in its principal place of business.

Considerations for choosing an entity type come down to the liability afforded, how owners are classified, and the type of taxation desired. The formal components of a corporation are the articles of incorporation and the bylaws (called "Operating Agreements" in an LLC). The bylaws are where the cooperative structure is able to define itself, especially if an entity type other than a cooperative corporation is selected (see fig. 4).

Articles of incorporation is the paperwork filed with the secretary of state forming the legal establishment of a business as a corporate entity. If one chooses to not incorporate a business, there is no legal separation between the business and its owners, leaving owners vulnerable to a multitude of risks, including to their personal assets. Additionally, incorporation allows for businesses to apply for loans, to obtain lines of credit, and to open bank accounts. Rules regarding Articles of incorporation vary from state to state, but there are general requirements for what information is included in these documents.[134] Typically states will require the following:

- business name
- principal office address
- general purpose of business
- duration of corporation if it does not operate in perpetuity
- name and address of the registered agent (someone who accepts service of lawsuits and other important documentation on behalf of the business)
- initial board of directors
- number and type of stocks
- name and addresses of incorporators (founders)

These articles must be submitted to the state filing agency, and once they are accepted, the business will receive a certificate formally recognizing it as a legal entity. These articles are updated annually.

The bylaws define cooperative principles. However, there is no one set of bylaws that will work for every organization. Bylaws should be tailored to meet an organization's legal requirements.[135] States often require that bylaws be drafted, but they are not filed with the government and are not legally binding. However, worker-owners operate as though these bylaws *are* legally binding; they outline the agreed-upon internal code of ethics. Many cooperatives publish their bylaws

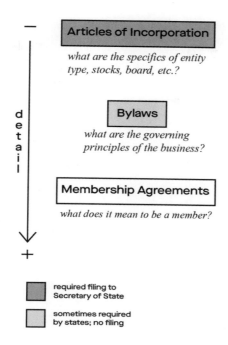

Corporations require legal documentation to incorporate. The documents filed with the state give only a vague, big-picture overview of the corporate entity, as compared to the detailed internal documents that describe day-to-day firm operations.

on their website, both for the sake of transparency, and to demonstrate solidarity with other cooperatives. A cooperative's bylaws are its operational guidelines for governance, and often include the following:[136]

- membership requirements including responsibilities for members
- membership application process
- membership expulsion process with exit strategy—how and when the exiting members' equity will be distributed
- governance and meeting procedures including voting requirements and procedures, the process for electing officers of the board, officers' term limits, duties, etc.
- time and place of directors' meetings
- fiscal year dates
- surplus distributions process, cycle length, and requirement
- amount of retained earnings
- procedures for losses
- dissolution process
- indemnity of owners
- process to amend the bylaws

Bylaws require decisions about a co-op's governance and hierarchy to be made. Beyond the clause "one worker, one vote," co-ops need to define when all members must be assembled to make decisions and when the board or various subcommittees can make decisions on behalf of the organization. Decisions voted on by the membership will include instances wherein workers' lives are directly affected, such as changes to salary or work hours.

Cooperative boards can either be collective, such that all members are on the board or elected by the membership. Collective boards are often present in smaller coops, while elected boards are common in larger ones. If the organization is large enough, a subcommittee or working group structure may be a sensible way to siphon certain decisions away from the board in order to reduce their consolidated power and disperse decisions among more worker-owners.

Cooperative bylaws must define *how* decisions are made democratically. The recommended methodology varies based on the size of the organization and the desires of its members. One decision making method used by many cooperatives is consensus, such that no worker objects to the decision or proposal being voted on. Consensus in this case does not mean that everyone necessarily agrees with the decision; rather, consensus refers to the lack of objection. This process can be tiresome and is sometimes mitigated by requiring only two-thirds of all members, for example, to reach consensus.

A democratic governance methodology that is gaining credence among cooperatives is "sociocracy." The organizational structure of a sociocracy is based on circles or small groups. These circles are interconnected, with members acting as liaisons between circles. Meeting structure is rigorously defined, and every member is encouraged to share an opinion prior to a vote. This is notable because in other decision-making processes, those with a louder voice tend to dominate discussions, leaving quieter members to feel disenfranchised by the organization. The consent-based decision-making model set forth in a sociocracy intends to break down this dynamic and empower all members.

To be clear, governance is not the same as firm management. Firms can still operate with an internal hierarchy even if every worker is an owner, though smaller firms might be interested in a more horizontal structure. The difference is that workers are included in governance decisions, and there is transparency regarding firm operations.

Some cooperatives use bylaws to outline the basic structure of governance but utilize resolutions by the board to address specific policy and operational changes. Examples include amendments to the owner handbook, "buy-in" fee structure changes, and a change to voting procedures. Early in the life of the cooperative these may change quite frequently, as there is no one set of bylaws that can address the needs of each unique organization.

Membership agreements are not required, but many co-ops choose to utilize them as "contracts," separate from the bylaws, that worker-owners agree to upon formalizing their membership. This document can describe in more detail membership shares, initial capital contributions (member equity), patronage dividends (how surplus is distributed at the end of the fiscal year), and termination of membership.[137] These documents should be reviewed by the entire membership.

Sub T, Sub S, and Sub K[138]

Upon incorporation, every legal entity type defaults to a specific taxation sub-chapter of the Internal Revenue Code (IRC), issued by the Internal Revenue Service (IRS). For example, a common corporation defaults to subchapter C. However, most entity types (with the exception of the sole proprietorship) can elect a different taxation strategy through forms offered by the IRS. For example, common corporations can elect to use subchapter S (thus acting as an "S Corporation") instead of subchapter C. The code also allows LLCs to elect sub-chapter T (the cooperative subchapter), instead of defaulting to subchapter K.

There are advantages and disadvantages for each taxation strategy. Depending on the number of owners in an organization and its expected profits, a particular taxation subchapter may be advisable. One should work with an attorney and a CPA to select the best taxation strategy for the organization.[139]

Subchapter C

C corporations are subject to double taxation as the entity pays taxes on its net earnings (profits), and shareholders pay income taxes on distributed ordinary dividends from those earnings.[140] The corporate tax rate is lower than the rate for individuals. C Corporations can accrue reserves, meaning money can be set aside within the corporation for future use, and ultimately the corporation becomes an asset. Money directed toward reserves is not taxed until it is distributed as wages, bonuses, or dividends. This structure is considered disadvantageous for smaller organizations because tight profit margins make double taxation more damaging. However, depending on the income of shareholders (which determines at what tax bracket they will be assessed) and the profits of the company (which can be reduced by directing money toward reserves), double taxation may be advantageous.

Subchapter S

S corporations do not pay corporate taxes. As "pass through" tax entities, owners are taxed directly on the profits of the organization. This may be advantageous given the amount of profits expected and the income bracket of the owners. A common S corporation strategy is to maintain relatively low owners' wages (which lowers payroll taxes and the applicable tax bracket of the owner) and relatively high profit margins at the end of the fiscal year. Profit is allocated to owners who then pay income taxes at a relatively low-income tax rate. Profit allocation of an S corporation is not subject to self-employment tax.

Anyone with a more than 2 percent share of an S corporation is considered an owner, and any benefits paid by the corporation are included in owners' wages. Additionally, S corporations receive the qualified business income (QBI) tax deduction, which allows owners to deduct up to 20 percent of their qualified business income from their personal income taxes.[141] Income from a C corporation is not eligible for this deduction.

There are requirements and restrictions inherent to S corporations that impact the decision to utilize this tax strategy. First, ownership is limited to US

Citizens. Second, there is only one class of stock available, meaning profits and losses must be based on the proportion of shares held, and there are no "voting-only" shares available. This is a disadvantage for some owners because of "Founders Syndrome," a situation in which the founders believe the organization to be eternally indebted to them for their initial sweat equity. Founders often want their own separate shares that weigh more than other owners' shares, either for voting or profit sharing, which is anathema to the cooperative spirit of "one worker, one vote." In an S corporation it is possible for one or more owners to hold a greater number of shares than others, however, when modifying this model's bylaws in order to be cooperative, it's important to limit the extent of shareholding differential to prevent any single owner from having too much financial or governing power.

Because of the pass-through nature of the S corporation, it cannot legally maintain reserves—meaning that the firm as an entity is unable to build equity. At the end of the year, all profits are allocated (not necessarily distributed) to the owners' internal capital accounts. Owners pay personal income tax on their share (portion) of profits upon allocation. The bylaws describe what happens to this money once it's allocated. It can either be distributed immediately or kept in the company's account for a certain amount of time (say, three years) to help with cashflow purposes, effectively acting as the "reserves" of the corporation, as is common with many start-up cooperatives. The main difference between this model and the workings of a C corporation is that the money is earmarked for a specific owner and taxes have already been paid on it. Should an owner decide to leave the company, that money must be distributed to them (the amount and timeframe for distribution is specified in the bylaws). There is a lot of nuance here, and care should be taken to protect both the cashflow of the business and the net earnings of any owner.

Subchapter T

Subchapter T is commonly considered the cooperative taxation strategy, outside of cooperative statutes. T corporations are applicable to a broad range of businesses, including cooperatives, though worker cooperatives are not explicitly mentioned in the revenue code.[142] The IRS defines businesses operating on "a cooperative basis" as democratic (one owner, one vote) and equitable (profits are distributed by value or quantity of service, like hours, rather than by share that can vary in weight for voting or profit sharing).[143]

This tax election combines a number of benefits from subchapters S and C. Income allocated through qualified "patronage" dividends is not doubly taxed, rather it is passed through directly to the owner. The reserves are taxed at the entity level—the lower corporate rate. However, income that is allocated for wages, or on a non-patronage basis, is doubly taxed. There are ways to navigate these rules to maximize benefit for the organization.

A disadvantage of subchapter T is that certain states restrict its use to particular types of businesses, so depending on your jurisdiction, it's not always available. Additionally, subchapter T is not as common as other subchapters, and not all CPAs are familiar with it.

Subchapter K

Partnerships, LLPs, and LLCs default to this subchapter, but are able to elect an alternative taxation strategy. Subchapter K entities don't pay taxes—owners pay them at the self-employment tax rate. Some accountants consider this a complicated form of taxation, because all transactions must be allocated, and there are comparatively many more rules than for other subchapters.

Taxation strategies are complex, and it ultimately requires both an attorney and a CPA to confirm that a business entity type is compatible with a desired taxation strategy. Taxation strategy decision should consider the projected income of the office, the salary of the owners, the employment status of owners, and how important reserves are for the well-being of the organization.

SALARIES AND PATRONAGE

Many worker cooperatives maintain flat salaries across all worker-owners, but it is possible to entertain varied salaries as in a traditional business. In this scenario, bylaws often specify a ratio cap between the highest- and lowest-paid employee. A common ratio is 3:1, wherein the highest paid worker can receive no more than three times the salary of the lowest paid earner. This ratio ensures that a worker-owner cannot disproportionately accrue financial power over other workers, which might lead to resentment within the office. All salaries, and any changes to them, should require a discussion and a vote from all worker-owners.

Another way that worker-owners receive money from co-ops is through patronage dividends. Patronage is the basis of how surplus (net income generated directly by owners as opposed to employees) is allocated at the end of the year; it's a measurement of a worker-owner's value contribution to the cooperative. Worker-cooperatives commonly allocate surplus based on the number of hours worked in a given year. The calculation of hours worked can be weighted to correspond to the salary of the member-owner, meaning higher-paid individuals can receive a higher proportion of surplus than those with lower salaries. Alternatively, salaries might vary while surplus is split evenly among all owners.

Allocation means that surplus money is "applied" to the internal capital accounting of the member-owners, i.e., retained earnings. The actual distribution, or payout, happens at regular intervals per a schedule set forth in the bylaws. The schedule is typically staggered two or three years out from the year that it is allocated. For example, profits from fiscal year 2020 would be allocated at the end of the 2020 tax year, but money would not be distributed to the worker until 2022 or 2023. It's important for co-ops to retain this money, especially in their early years, for cash flow purposes (see fig. 5).

	2020	2021	2022	2023
W/O 1				
Allocation	+1000	-800	+5000	+7000
Distribution	+500	+1000	+1500	+1000
W/O 2				
Allocation	+1800	-1000	+8000	+7000
Distribution	+500	+1000	+2000	+1800
W/O 3				
Allocation	+100	-800	+4500	+7000
Distribution	+500	+1000	+800	+100

Model allocation and distribution schedule showing a three-year distribution cycle. Some cooperatives choose this extended cycle for cash flow purposes, retaining revenue in internal accounts.

ARCHITECTS

A combination of strategies can be used to cooperativize an architectural firm. It will take careful planning and consultation with an attorney to identify the best path forward for a particular business. Architects—few of whom think about cooperatives at all—tend to believe that the legally recognized cooperative entity type is the only "true" definition of a cooperative. By using different entity types in combination with strategic use of the US tax code, there are many ways an office can define itself as a cooperative without relying on cooperative statutes.

Further complicating decisions regarding entity types is the fact that architects are considered professionals. States regulate professional licensure to protect consumers and resist corporate entity types that assume equality between those with a license and those without. Each state has its own set of regulations, and some explicitly prohibit architects from using certain entity types, for example, architects cannot incorporate as an LLC in the state of California.

The conflict between professional incorporation laws and cooperative entity types is amply demonstrated in the state of California. Architects must incorporate as general corporations, or into the subset of professional corporations. The California Cooperative Corporation type does not fall under the general corporation umbrella, and therefore professionals are not able to utilize this statute (see fig. 6).

In the instance that an organization wants to incorporate out of state—for example if using a cooperative corporation statute is a priority for the organization, and their home state does not provide this option—they can register as a foreign

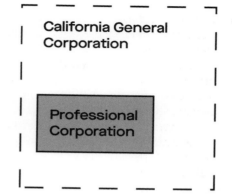

California Cooperative Corporation

California General Corporation

Professional Corporation

The California Business and Professions Code stipulates that architects and other professionals must incorporate under General Corporation Statutes rather than as LLCs, LLPs, or coops.

entity in their state of business. As reviewed previously, this creates additional risk for the business, as it can be subject to litigation in both states: the state in which it incorporates, and the state in which it practices. In addition, owners need to check with their secretary of state and licensing board to understand any additional regulation regarding out-of-state incorporation within the profession. Colorado is considered the mecca for cooperative incorporation, as it hosts a suite of cooperative statutes that the state has been developing for over fifty years.[144]

Once an entity type is selected, the choice of taxation strategy follows. In 2019, the AIA found that the most common entity type for architecture offices is the S corporation, representing 35 percent of all firms.[145] For small offices, subchapter S avoids double taxation, taxing owners at their personal tax bracket, while not taxing the corporation. This is important in industries with very tight profit margins, like architecture. While intended for cooperative businesses, applying subchapter T to an architecture firm could actually be disadvantageous given anticipated wage to profit ratios. A certified CPA will be able to recommend the best tax strategy.

Bylaws are rarely tailored to a specific industry, but rather describe the meta-level operation of a business. A method of governance must be established for any given firm. A popular governance strategy among cooperatives is modified consensus. It should be noted that transparency and democratic participation in firm governance via membership does not mean that design decisions, like window placement, require a membership vote. Voting is required only for decisions that affect the firm's operation as a whole, not for day-to-day decisions about work product. The firm's design process is not described in the bylaws unless, of course, the office chooses it to be, in which case a clause can be added.

It is important to determine how a cooperative architecture firm calculates patronage. Because most architecture firms are likely to incorporate with a statute other than a cooperative corporation statute, this affords some flexibility regarding patronage calculations. Some creative alternatives to the hourly work

44 basis for patronage can be considered. This is particularly relevant for firms with a strong horizontal structure, and relatively flat salaries. Owners in small firms often end up wearing many hats, working a different number of hours at different intensities on different projects. This makes hourly work a challenging basis for patronage, especially if one owner feels they have put in more effort than another because of, say, a difficult client, whether or not that effort is reflected in the number of hours worked.

An alternative method to determine patronage is to combine an hourly base with a multiplier. The multiplier could be applied to tricky clients, or to specific hourly tasks that are especially draining. Members should feel that their hard work is being rewarded. Another strategy is a point system whereby certain tasks are ranked using a set point allocation procedure. [146] Perhaps production work is ranked at one point, while correspondence with a very needy client is ranked at five points. At the end of the year, patronage would be calculated based on the number of points a member-owner accrues.

Ultimately, the firm should manage how work is divided, and no single worker should feel exploited at any time. However, there are always variations to considered. Any patronage system should be agreed upon by all members and tested for a fixed amount of time (at least one year). Do workers who believe they had a harder task on a given project feel that this system works for them? Do workers feel rewarded for their hard work?

Finally, since architecture licenses are associated with an individual rather than a business, it's important to clarify that cooperatives are corporations and are therefore entitled to all the corporate protections of limited liability. This is one of the strongest arguments to incorporate an office rather than remain an unincorporated collection of practitioners. Firms with multiple licensed owners might want to create a strategy for the distribution of stamping. Projects would receive a rating based on risk, and with high risk, the role of stamping would rotate. Or there could be a single architect stamping all projects. This depends on how the firm wants to handle the professional obligations that come with stamping, which are linked to the individual practitioner. The limited liability protection that derives from the corporate entity type (alongside insurance) should protect the stamping architect from direct liability but will not prevent entanglement in any given lawsuit. Additionally, some architects feel that being the stamping architect, the Architect of Record, contributes to their participation in ownership of a given office. Therefore, it's important to determine how best to distribute this responsibility.

EMPLOYEE STOCK OWNERSHIP PLANS (ESOPs)

As previously stated, ESOPs are an employee benefit plan that can be used to transfer full or partial ownership, or profits from the company, to employees. Stock shares are held in trust and administered by a trustee (elected by the board) on the employees' behalf. Employee shareholders typically do not have any governance or management control over the operations of the plan itself. Federal laws govern how ESOPs are administered, granting employees voting rights on certain issues, such as the sale of company assets or the dissolution of the company.

However, employees do not necessarily vote for the board of directors, nor do they have a say on (or transparent access to) any of the firm's policies.[147] Essentially, ESOPs benefit employees when they retire, not before, and are used to incentivize employees to remain at the firm as the value of their shares increases over time.

There are ways to create democratic ESOPs, wherein employee shareholders elect the board of directors and vote on shareholder matters, but this model is rare. In a democratic ESOP model, the employee shareholders direct the trustee on voting matters, but votes are not passed down to employee shareholders. This is a complex governance method, utilized by only a handful of ESOPs, albeit one that allows for greater democratic control of a corporation for firms looking to operate more cooperatively.[148]

While ESOPs are an enticing model for firm owners looking to give their employees a sense of ownership, and while owners benefit from the tax deductions inherent to the model, they are not, to reiterate, cooperatives. Being able to market a firm as "100 percent Employee-Owned" is misleading, since most ESOPs fail to offer democratic governance to participating employees, which is the keystone of the cooperative model, and implied in the notion of ownership. The moniker "employee-owned" does not necessarily mean "employee-controlled" (see fig. 7).

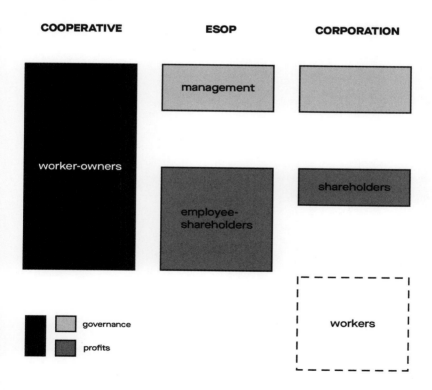

While firms with ESOPS are often described as "employee-owned," an ESOP is just a profit sharing program and has no relation to employee ownership or firm governance.

While entity types and taxation strategies may seem dry, understanding these details supports the formation and creation of more democratic workplaces, and worker empowerment in general. The lack of education around the cooperative model is a shortcoming of architectural academia; if professional practice courses were more aspirational for our future architects, this text would not be necessary. Yes, legislation on professional cooperatives varies from state to state, making cooperativization challenging for architects to interpret. Yes, there is no one solution for all offices. Nevertheless it is increasingly possible to find a pathway to coopertivization, as more and more organizations are created that aid firms—architectural and otherwise—who want to avoid standard, depleting, and precarious worker exploitation. Several resources are currently available for cooperative incorporation and transition (see the appendix). There are also funding opportunities available for incorporation efforts, and many cooperative-friendly attorneys are willing to provide their services pro bono. Likewise, legislation continues to be advanced that supports the formation of more cooperatives at the local, state, and national level. Architects can both take advantage of these efforts and support them by looking beyond the profession's limited silo to the labor movement at large.

Part III
Interview with South
Mountain Company

In 2020, I spoke with John Abrams, Deirdre Bohan, and Abbie Zelle, some of the worker-owners of South Mountain Company (SMCo), an architecture firm founded in 1975 and cooperativized in 1987 in West Tisbury, Martha's Vineyard, Massachusetts. John is the co-author of *Companies We Keep* (2008), a book about employee ownership.[149] Deirdre has been with SMCo since 1995. As the longest standing architectural cooperative in the United States, the organization's guiding principles were worthy of discussion. I was curious to understand their initial decisions, moments of growth, and challenges to the co-op model from the point of view of a firm that has proven that model successful for many years. To that end, John and Deirdre introduced me to a new owner, Abbie Zelle, to share her perspective on their ownership process and on how SMCo differs from other architecture firms.

The following interview has been edited and condensed.

ASHTON HAMM
John, [in *Companies We Keep*] you expressed a tension in your initial decision of cooperativizing—the fear of losing control versus the value of extending ownership and sharing responsibility. I'm curious, do you think that the decision to cooperativize would've been more challenging later on?

JOHN ABRAMS
I really don't. I think it can be successfully done at any stage of a company's development and maturation. We were lucky to do it early. We did it with very little knowledge or understanding of the significance of what we were doing. (We didn't know what the hell we were doing!) Transitioning early gave us decades of first-generation time to discover and refine our approach, but many companies do successfully convert to a worker co-op when the founder's ready to retire. Many of the current transitions to worker co-ops are occurring because of baby boomers. They've put thirty or forty years of heart and soul into their business, are ready to retire, and considering what's next. Converting to a worker co-op has become a more common entity of choice.

AH

I want to dispel some of the misconceptions that all cooperatives are hierarchy-less and horizontally organized, and workers sit in meetings all the time. I attended a panel hosted by DAWI [Democracy at Work Institute] a few months ago where you showed your org chart with distinct hierarchies. I'm wondering if you could provide some examples of your internal hierarchy and how it functions.

JA

We believe in a hierarchy of expertise rather than a hierarchy of power. We want the people who are best prepared to make decisions to make the decisions. We don't sit around and draw straws. We do have a hierarchy, but we're always balancing inclusivity and collaboration with efficiency and effectiveness. It's a lifelong exploration how to figure out the best balance. Our project architects have a lot of freedom to design and conduct the process and the client relationship, but it's not without intense collaboration and supervision. Each project is a series of understandings that we craft together.

As to the notion of sitting in meetings forever: we have, and need, many meetings, but they are highly productive. We have spent a tremendous amount of time learning about meeting facilitation. We are rigorous about agendas and times, and minutes. All of that is very structured and we're learning more all the time.

AH

So you use consensus for decision making. I'm curious, how did that develop over time? Have you always used this method of decision making, or have you tried a few others?

JA

Our owners use consensus decision-making for policy matters. But we have a backup voting mechanism, a super majority of 75 percent. If there's a stalemate and we can't reach consensus, then we can vote. We have used this three times in thirty-something years. So it doesn't happen very often.

Deirdre Bohan

And if we can't come to some kind of agreement, we just push the decision for a week or two. Maybe we don't have enough information. Maybe people need to think about it some more. Instead of rushing to make it a decision that perhaps not everyone agrees with, we just take the time. And I think the difference is, again, what John's talking about, is that our architecture practice is not run by consensus. What's really run by consensus is our policy. The rest is run in a more traditional way. However, it's largely collaborative.

AH

Can you share a bit of insight into how democratic decision making plays out in the architecture team? I'm sure you have staff from other companies that are used to taking orders from above only.

Our management decisions have traditionally been very collaborative, but not without management and supervision. Architects who come from other firms say that the difference is significant. It feels different. They're kind of amazed that it can work that way and excited by how well it does work. They're working across disciplines. We have architecture, engineering, building interior design, and solar in house and collaborate with many external consultants. The project architects lead that process and have a lot of freedom, but if something is veering off the path, it gets pulled back. If the budget, for example, does not align with the design, there are checks and balances. The consultants are woven into the process and become full members of the team, especially landscape architects. That shows up in a kind of coherence, which marries the program, aesthetics, and performance. It feels to us like a system that produces better buildings.

AH

How is patronage determined at South Mountain?

JA

It's really simple. Everybody has a wage or salary. You get paid that money or a salary that is part of organized wage scales and aligned with our org chart. At the end of the year, we have a net income, and approximately 35 percent of that gets distributed to every person in the company based on hours worked. This partially mitigates the hierarchical wage scale. Roughly half of what remains gets distributed as patronage (also by hours worked).

AH

I also read that you hold retained earnings within the company and there's a different fund that you're putting money into that could even provide loans for housing for your employees?

DB

These are two different things—ownership patronage and housing grants. As John mentioned, we distribute annual patronage to the owners in the form of a cash dividend and a note payable upon leaving the company. At this time, you can get 100 percent of your equity balance if you take it over eight years and it's a sliding scale from there—for example, if you take it five years, you get a little bit less.

Since many owners spend their careers here, we want to ensure we can meet our financial obligations for that note payable to them upon retirement so we backup the equity with a cash investment account equal to about 50 to 60 percent of the total equity value. Once a year, we rebalance the account and plan for upcoming retirements.

The housing grant is one of our Operating Policies and Benefits, one where we contribute to an employee who is buying or renovating their primary residence. It's intended as a financial leg-up, and often fellow employees will contribute their time and expertise too.

Our operating policy document is worth a look. It codifies the many ways we try to support our staff at all stages of life. Financial wellbeing, 100 percent health insurance, electric vehicle subsidies, tool allowances, and more … the list is long.

JA
The equity now amounts to millions of dollars. That's an obligation of the company to former owners. In the past decade, a half a dozen first-generation owners, who in combination worked for about 180 years have departed. So we're always paying off many people. The younger people who are currently accumulating equity are likewise expecting it to be there when they retire. So we're managing this backup money all the time, kind of like social security, with a twenty-five year spreadsheet that has built-in assumptions. And we try to do the best that we can. We manage this fund to assure there will be enough to satisfy future need.

AH
Can you share a little bit of perspective on the ownership process? I understand that it takes about five years. There are a lot of changes between day one of employment versus five years in. Are there people that come to you without knowledge of employee ownership? And has it posed issues with workers who joined the company and not being prepared to become owners at the end of that five years?

JA
When we hire, we explain the ownership system and the five-year Path to Ownership. It's an appealing part of the overall package. You don't have to become an owner just because you're eligible. Most people do, although some not right away, for financial and family reasons. Some people do it many years after they're eligible. And some people, very few, never do it. So there's no obligation, but there is a culture of expectation. Both the financial rewards and the voice and vote are very attractive. We have good payment terms to make it less onerous.

Abbie Zell
I just became an owner in 2019 after coming on as an intern right after college and spending about six years here. I was grateful for that longer runway leading up to eligibility.

Not only did it allow me to save the money at a manageable pace, but all that time to just observe fostered a real reverence. After five years of steeping in this culture, the shift felt a lot more meaningful. South Mountain's really intentional about preparing new hires for the responsibility of taking on and succeeding at ownership. I was groomed through what was an unspoken process that we're now formalizing into a program called the Path to Ownership. Think of it like a girl scout sash. You gain a badge for every experience, like learning how to read a balance sheet or mastering the company elevator pitch or spending a day out on the job site if your job is traditionally in the office. Once you have all the badges, you're ready to become a troop leader. It's a very well-thought-out process, and like John said, our culture promotes it.

AH

I'm curious about worker autonomy and ownership and how it has played out in the success of the business. But have you seen a transformation in workers once they become owners of this kind of desire towards ownership or have you seen the business bloom in a different way?

JA

There's no doubt that being an owner gives a certain kind of pride, greater commitment, more dedication. It means something when people can go out on the street and say, yeah, that's my company. Ownership is a big deal.

The transformation that happens over the five-year Path to Ownership leads to dedicated and effective members of the team who own their work, feel included, and have experienced the joys, tensions, challenges, and depth of working in a democratic workplace. I think it changes people and their relation to their work and their colleagues.

AH

Is there an expectation that your owners bring in a certain percentage of billings or a commitment towards project acquisition?

JA

People are not expected to bring work in except those whose job it is to do so. That being said, many people, through their connections and networks, bring work to the company. Profit sharing and dividends are based on the hours you are contributing to the overall success of the company, not to the direct revenue you're generating.

AH

I'm curious about your number of worker-owners. I've heard that the ideal worker cooperative sizes between three and twenty people. I think that you guys are over twenty. Did you feel any like strain or stresses growing beyond twenty, do you think that you could get even bigger, and it would still work great?

JA

We're thirty-eight [people]. Personally, I don't think size matters at all. I do think that conscious growth and adjustments to that growth are essential to really pay attention to because growth, brings challenges to all companies, whether they're democratic or not.

AH

So on the legal level, there's a lot of inconsistencies around how cooperatives are legislated between States. You all have found a way to become a cooperative corporation, and you're also a B corporation. So thinking about this as, as a larger movement, what do you think the pinch points are and a legislative issue or the legislative agenda that would help this?

JA

It's more of a mindset change than a legal one. The cooperative structure can help to alter the priesthood mentality that the architecture industry suffers from. Architectural education and company culture promotes this idea of priesthood and does not always promote collaboration and team mentality. The specific legal issues of becoming a cooperative can be easily managed by working with good consultants, attorneys, accountants, and other worker-owned companies.

AH

I'm curious how South Mountain did in 2008, and then how it's doing now with the pandemic?

JA

I often say that 2008 was the second-best thing that ever happened to us as a company because it was threatening, and it was unclear at first how we were going to survive. Everybody pulled together, we successfully managed our way through it, and we thrived. We vowed that we would never be in such a tenuous position again. At that point, we started creating a reserve fund for the next big economic challenge and that served us exceedingly well when this pandemic came.

DB

During the pandemic our strength as a group really came through. Everyone was in it together, looking out for the colleagues, understanding the variability in each person's experience and happy to be a member of a strong organization that puts them first.

AH

I understand John is about to retire. It sounds like his role is going to be split between several members. Where do you see South Mountain in the coming years?

JA

First, about the leadership: there are four department directors, and Deirdre will take my job as CEO. This extraordinarily well-aligned group of five will become (already has) our leadership team.

DB

It's really a continuation of the way we've been working for at least the last five years, so it seems very comfortable to us. John will transition out two years from now into a founder role, and he'll still be associated with the company and on call for what we need. In the meantime, we still have plenty of time left for planning and practice!

At this particular moment in time, it's really hard to think beyond [the pandemic]. I can imagine we're going to continue to do what we're doing: we're just going to be stronger and better at it!

AZ

We're a very nimble company, so we may add services or discontinue them. I don't know what that portfolio is going to look like, but I feel confident that we'll be here and just continuing to hone the craft of doing business, taking care of each other, and trying to make a meaningful difference in the world. As John said earlier, those values are just part of our DNA. They aren't going anywhere.

JA

Hey, if we can do that, that sounds pretty good. I'm excited because I feel like I'm leaving this company in what is clearly the best condition that it's ever been in. It's an astonishing group of people. And after those multiple first-generation retirements in the last five-to-ten years, we have been blessed to be able to welcome in a really passionate group of next-generation leaders and owners.

Conclusion

The profession of architecture has long separated itself from the labor movement. In fact, the profession has worked to isolate itself within the professional class and eschew the very notion of labor, leading to structural inequities, bad labor practices, and unhappy workers. As the horrors of late-stage capitalism play out around us, now is the time for architects to embrace the labor movement and advocate for themselves as workers. The worker-cooperative model offers a solution. For an industry like architecture that requires collaboration and coordination between many parties, cooperation should seem like an easy first step. However, the profession's origin in exclusionary and elitist practices has proven to be a great hurdle to this conclusion.

The legal challenges and technical obscurities involved in forming architectural cooperatives should not be dismissed. For those who have come to the cooperative solution, the task of navigating various states' Business and Professions Codes and talking to attorneys familiar neither with the profession nor the cooperative model, might seem like a dead end. However, it is increasingly possible to form an architectural cooperative either through cooperative statutes or by tailoring bylaws. It is also very possible to form cooperative networks with other interested architects—to share both the burdens that make running a small firm so challenging and the resources that can alleviate them.

Movements of solidarity, away from capitalist extraction, are happening around the globe in an effort to transition the economy toward a more just and sustainable model. Worker cooperatives form the keystone of these movements. Cooperatives keep money circulating in the local economy. Cooperatives support other cooperatives. Cooperatives care about their workers and actively work toward their collective prosperity in and outside of the workplace. Cooperative architects can play a role in this transition, creating the built spaces where cooperation happens, thereby transforming communities from within the framework of a cooperative understanding, working with partners who operate similarly. Cooperative practices attract clients with an interest in alternative modes of development such as Community Land Trusts, cooperative housing, businesses, and other community-oriented programs. Now is the time to get involved. This text, and the resources listed in the appendix, are meant as a push toward action.

Postscript

Since starting uxo architects in 2016, there have been—as there are with young practices—many ups and downs. It's been difficult to get established while going through location changes, ownership changes, and a global pandemic. Nevertheless, we've remained committed to the cooperative structure and are excited to see it carry us forward in the coming years through changes and growth. Already, when bringing in new people, our commitment to transparency in governance and finances and the desire to hire owners, not short-term employees, has proved the great benefit of the model. In our experience so far, limited as it may be, people interested in joining uxo architects are motivated to understand the inner workings of the office: they immediately want to participate as an active owner, making big decisions. It's hard to force that type of enthusiasm on someone who is just interested in a paycheck. Providing employees a clear, transparent path toward ownership and participation in the operational work that keeps the office running gives them the whole picture, up front, of what type of organization they will be joining should they become worker-owners. To see clearly how to move up and what future responsibilities will entail has proven motivating, especially for those coming from more traditional offices that often have obscure, subjective, and closed hierarchical ladders.

As we have increasingly committed to working with other cooperatives and community movements, we've also expanded our role as architects. Beyond mere service providers, we're running community engagement efforts, working with our clients to apply for grants to build organizational capacity, and stewarding strategic visioning sessions. We want their prosperity as much as they want ours.

Since 2020, we have been in many, many conversations with colleagues and those interested in the cooperative model. It has been an exciting turn to see the model gain interest and momentum. I've been invited to discuss the cooperative model in various college courses (including professional practice) from the University of Toronto to the University of California, San Diego. It's critical to introduce this alternative model of practice in schools. We must lay the groundwork for students to realize that they and their work are valuable and demystify the culture of "dues paying." I think it's important to remind architects entering the profession that they do not have to opt into defaults, they can practice *practice*. I hope this momentum is indicative of a strong future for the cooperative model within the design professions.

As I mentioned previously, my early interest in cooperatives was enhanced by my participation in The Architecture Lobby. Its Cooperative Network group

58 continues to offer support and advice to firms wanting to form cooperatives corporations and cooperative networks. The Lobby hosts workshops, firm-to-firm facilitations, and provides resources to those interested in incorporation. This book might tell you the bulk of what you need to know to cooperativize, but The Lobby offers connections to other individuals who worry about, and work through, the same struggles we've had to establish equitable practices. I'd like to thank The Lobby and especially Peggy Deamer for her encouragement in the publication of this book.

Appendix

Glossary

Allocation:
The assignment of money (gains or losses) to a particular worker-owner's internal capital account within the company's bank account. See *Distribution, Internal Capital Account.*

Articles of Incorporation:
The documents filed with the secretary of state to legally define the business entity.

Board of Directors:
The governing body of a company. In a cooperative this board is either elected by the membership or collective whereby all members are on the board.

Business and Professions Codes:
Each state has their own codes regulating businesses. These define how professions (like lawyers, doctors, architects, etc.) are regulated within the state.

Bylaws:
The document defining a firm's governance and organizational operations.

Capital Contribution:
Also called "buy-in," this is money that an owner pays to buy stocks. This money sits in an equity account separate from the retained patronage account. This money could increase in value if the company goes through a valuation process.

Cooperative Statute:
An entity type defining a cooperative business. These vary by state.

Consensus:
General agreement, or unanimity. This can be challenging, and even undesirable to achieve in a cooperative, as dissent is also important. Oftentimes, organizations will use Modified Consensus which allows for a ratio of less than 100 percent unanimity. A common ratio is two-thirds.

Corporate Tax Rate:
The tax rate applied to corporations. There is a federal rate as well as a state rate (for most states).

Corporation (S and C):
A business entity type in which stocks are purchased to own a portion of the company. These corporations operate to benefit shareholders.

Certified Public Accountant
(CPA): A licensed accountant.

Distribution:
Payout in actual money from internal capital accounts to worker-owners.

Equity:
The capital interest of any owner in the company. This includes initial investment plus any allocated gains or losses.

Fiscal Year:
The year that an organization chooses to measure its books. Some businesses choose to offset their fiscal year (from June to May, for example) in order to keep up with seasonal fluctuations that affect their business.

Governance:
How a firm's decisions are made.

Indemnity:
Security against loss. In contract law it is a clause for one party to hold the other harmless.

Internal Capital Account:
A bookkeeping method to track the equity of each owner.

Internal Revenue Code (IRC):
The tax code of the United States.

International Cooperative Alliance (ICA):
An international, nongovernmental body, founded in 1895, that unites cooperatives around the world.

Limited Liability:
A legal status wherein a person's financial liability is limited to a certain extent, often to their investment in the entity.

LLC:
Limited Liability Company—a business entity that protects its shareholders from personal financial responsibility in case of a lawsuit. There can be a single owner of an LLC.

LLP:
Limited Liability Partnership—a partnership wherein each of the partners are protected from personal financial responsibility in case of a lawsuit. An LLP must have two or more partners.

Membership:
The worker-owners of the cooperative.

Membership shares:
Stock certificates, also called "buy-in." See *Capital Contribution.*

Officers:
The board members legally responsible for the business and for signing official documents, etc.

Operating Agreement:
The document that defines governance and organizational operations of a Limited Liability Corporation (LLC).

Pass-through:
A taxation status wherein the business entity is not taxed (to avoid paying the corporate tax rate), and all tax responsibility is passed through to the owners of the business.

Patronage Dividends:
The amount of money paid (allocated then distributed) to a worker-owner usually defined by hours worked or salary. These are qualified dividends that avoid double taxation.

Profits:
Net income (excess minus expenses and losses) attributable to non-owner labor, as opposed to *Surplus.*

Reserves:
A savings account within the business entity's books set aside for future use. Depending on the tax structure, a percentage of business revenue can be directed to the reserves account on a regular basis.

Retained Earnings:
Net income of a company that has been allocated to owners' internal capital accounts but not distributed. In an S corporation, this money has been taxed, but remains in the account for a given amount of time (per bylaws) for cashflow purposes.

Self-Employment Tax:
An additional tax, separate tax from income tax, paid by self-employed persons.

Sociocracy:
A method of governance that uses discussion and consent rather than consensus. All members voting must consent to the issue at hand, otherwise the issue must be modified. Consent in this case is defined to include a range of tolerance, e.g., "This issue may not benefit me personally, but I can live with it."

Stamping:
Referring to a licensed architect stamping their drawing set prior to submission. The stamp signifies that the architect has performed their work in accordance with a standard of care that another architect in a similar jurisdiction would perform.

Surplus:
Net income (excess minus expenses and losses) attributable to owner labor rather than employee labor.

Taxation Strategy:
The strategy a business chooses for its taxation, often with the aim of lowering its tax burden. This may include switching to an alternative subchapter that is more advantageous for the income bracket of the owners and the expected profit margins of the business.

Uniform Limited Cooperative Association Act:
This law creates a new business entity that is different from a cooperative corporation in that it allows for outside funding from investors. Currently, the act has been passed in Colorado, the District of Columbia, Kentucky, Nebraska, Oklahoma, Utah, Vermont, and Washington.

Uniform State Laws: Uniform laws are an attempt to pass a uniformly consistent laws at the state level for the purpose of better understanding between states.

Voting-Only Shares:
Ownership stock that gives more voting power, but not necessarily an additional percentage of ownership, to the shareholder. These shares are only available in certain entity types.

Worker-Owner:
The owners of the cooperative. Can also be called "the membership."

List of Resources for Cooperatives

GENERAL/DEVELOPMENT
- ICA Group
- Democracy at Work Institute (DAWI)
- The US Federation of Worker Cooperatives
- The Sustainable Economies Law Center (SELC)
- CA Center for Cooperative Development
- Co-op Law
- University of Wisconsin Center for Cooperatives
- The USDA

LEGAL ENTITIES
- Options for worker cooperatives:
  https://takerootjustice.org/wp-content/uploads/2019/06/FactSheet
  _Legal_Entity_Options_for_Worker_Cooperatives_201108.pdf

- Webinar: California Entity options for worker cooperatives:
  https://www.theselc.org/webinar_resources_ca_entity_options
  _for_worker_cooperatives

- Comparing business structures:
  https://resources.uwcc.wisc.edu/Legal/BusinessStructureComparison
  .pdf

- Choose an entity for worker cooperatives:
  https://www.theselc.org/how_to_choose_an_entity_for
  _your_cooperative

- Form a cooperative corporation:
  https://www.theselc.org/how_to_form_a_cooperative_corporation

NONPROFIT CO-OPS
- Worker self-directed nonprofits:
  https://www.theselc.org/worker_selfdirected_nonprofits

66   ·   Comparing nonprofits to cooperative entities:
https://resources.uwcc.wisc.edu/Legal/NonprofitCoopComparison
.pdf

HOW TO USE SUBCHAPTER T
·   Webinar: how to file taxes using subchapter T:
https://www.theselc.org/how_to_file_taxes_as_a_subchapter_t_cooperative

HOW TO FINANCE A WORKER COOPERATIVE
·   Webinar from the SELC:
https://www.theselc.org/how_to_finance_a_worker_cooperative

SAMPLE EMPLOYEE HANDBOOKS
·   For a cooperative corporation:
https://drive.google.com/file/d/1g6cLnnQD-c3-Q-RI9ptwoFYjdnABr4rG
/view

·   For an LLC or other entity:
https://drive.google.com/a/theselc.org
/file/d/1gLIoQeRckkDjg7_4_Eh8d4RhaPEQZJpq/view?usp=drivesdk

WORKER COOPERATIVE FRIENDLY 401K ALT
·   The Next Egg:
https://www.thenextegg.org

COOPERATIVE SUPPORT GROUPS/DEVELOPERS/FACILITATORS
·   Cooperation Works! is a cooperative development network with forty-two
members serving fifty states. Their website allows for a search per state:
https://cooperationworks.coop

·   Cultivate.coop lists cooperative developers by region in the United States,
Canada, and Internationally:
https://cultivate.coop/wiki/Cooperative_Developers

CPAS AND ATTORNEYS FAMILIAR
WITH PROFESSIONAL COOPERATIVES
·   The Cooperative Professionals Guild is a collective of attorneys and CPAs
familiar with cooperative legislation and membership across
the US:
https://www.professionals.coop

- Local cooperative networks will know of local attorneys familiar with cooperative statutes. Regionally, there are organizations that provide start-up resources. For example, the NYC Network of Worker Cooperatives (NYC-NOWC) and the State of New York created the program Owners to Owners NYC, which provides start-up support for transitioning or beginning worker cooperatives.

SAMPLE BYLAWS

- Bylaws need to be tailored to each organization. There are several "general" cooperative bylaw templates that can be found through an online search. The University of Wisconsin's Center for Cooperatives provides an outline and a guide:
  https://resources.uwcc.wisc.edu/Legal/SampleBylaws.pdf

- Another guide that is helpful to answer questions prior to writing bylaws is called, "28 Questions to Ask Before Meeting the Lawyer" and can be found here:
  https://institute.coop/sites/default/files/resources/28questionsBeforeMeetingLawyer.pdf

- Additionally, the Democracy at Work Institute provides sample bylaws for cooperative corporations:
  https://institute.coop/sites/default/files/SampleWorkerCooperativeBylaws.pdf

OTHER COOPERATIVE NETWORKS EXAMPLES

- ArchiTeam
- Nordic Works Collective
- LaCol Coop
- Labaula
- Voltes Cooperativa
- Assemble
- Pool Architekten
- La Borda
- La Ciutat Invisible
- Sostre Civic
- Coop57

US DEPARTMENT OF AGRICULTURE'S 10 COMMON PITFALLS FACED BY NEW COOPERATIVES150

- Lack of Clearly Identified Mission
- Inadequate Planning
- Failure to Use Experienced Advisors and Consultants
- Lack of Member Commitment
- Lack of Competent Management
- Failure to Identify and Minimize Risk

· Poor Assumptions
· Lack of Financing
· Inadequate Communications

CASE STUDY: NEW ERA WINDOWS

A recent example of the beneficial relationship between unions and cooperatives occurred in 2008 when Republic Windows and Doors in Chicago gave employees only three days' notice before it planned on shutting down. Bank of America had cut the company's line of credit due to the Great Recession. The company's announcement did not come with any guarantee of contract terms or pay outs for workers, and workers were nervous they would be left without pay, severance, or the continued benefits in their contract. This was in violation of the WARN Act, which requires workers to receive sixty days' notice before a factory closure. The workers were represented by a union, United Electrical, Radio, and Machine Workers of America (UE), Local 1110, and upon hearing of the closure members voted unanimously to occupy the factory in protest. The occupation worked—they were able to negotiate an agreement with Republic Windows and Doors and Bank of America guaranteeing them eight weeks of wages, including pay for unused vacation days and two months of healthcare.[151]

Subsequently, Republic Windows and Doors was purchased and reopened by Serious Energy, who sought to produce a low-carbon building product. The product failed to launch, and once again the factory was set to close its doors in 2012. The workers, some of whom were still UE Local 1110 members, organized another sit-in, hoping for a similar success. This time their goal was to negotiate for first right of refusal, meaning the workers could make an offer to purchase the business before other buyers. This strategy worked, and the workers won the right of first refusal to purchase the factory.

Workers needed to raise $1.1 million for the purchase. The union got word that Serious Energy had started negotiations with a liquidation firm, which violated the workers right to first refusal, and threatened legal action. The union then became aware of a second liquidation firm that was interested in Serious Energy's assets, approached them, and struck a deal to liquidate some assets while keeping others in order to lower the company's purchase price. The workers wanted to downsize the operation in order to create a sustainable worker co-op. The deal went through, and New Era Windows Cooperative has been in operation since 2012.[152]

ESOPs, CONTINUED

A study comparing ESOPS and cooperatives found that there is no reason to assume that ESOPs are more successful—in terms of employee benefits and share value—than cooperatives.[153] The study looks at patronage benefits, employee benefits, and company cash retention in both a high-growth and low-growth scenario. Those enrolled in the ESOP early on benefit more than those that join

after the loan is paid off.[154] However, the cooperative model share value increases   69
steadily over time, but patronage benefits are greater for those who join later in
the plan rather than early on. The study observes more factors than these, but in
summary, there is no clear leading advantage to the ESOP in terms of employee
benefits. The reason that this model is ubiquitous is the tax benefits it provides
companies and shareholders. And, of course, the marketable value of claiming
"employee ownership."

The cash and stock contributions are tax deductible. Loan repayment contributions for leveraged ESOPs[155] are also tax deductible. An S-Corporation ESOP
allows owners to deduct the percentage of income attributable to the ESOP from
their federal and sometimes state taxes. C-Corporation ESOPs allow owners
with 30 percent or more stock to defer taxation on their capital gains. Employees
are only taxed at the time of distribution, not contribution. They can use their
allowable retirement accounts or IRAs to roll these distributions into for further
tax benefits.[156]

These tax benefits make the ESOP an attractive model for companies with
the funds to support the administrative costs associated with the conversion
to an ESOP. It's no surprise that ESOPs outnumber cooperatives. In the United
States there are over 6,000 companies utilizing the ESOP model and 612 worker
cooperatives.[157] Before COVID, US ESOPs held $1.4 trillion in plan assets with
an average employee ownership stake of $130,000.[158] The largest ESOP business
in the United States is Publix Supermarkets with over 200,000 employees. The
National Center for Employee Ownership (NCEO) publishes a list annually of
the top 100 ESOP businesses in the United States. The largest architecture and
engineering firms on the list are: HDR, Inc with 100,000 employees, followed by
Burns & McDonnell Engineering with 6,650 employees and Gensler with 6,000
employees.[159] All three of these (ranking in 10, 16, and 21 place respectively) are
100 percent employee owned.

In observing the macroeconomic benefits of ESOPs, particularly S-corporation ESOPs (S-ESOPs) it is undeniable how vital they are to the economy. In 2010
S-ESOPs directly supported 470,000 jobs with $29 billion in income and aver-
age of $60,000 in salary. These companies had $93 billion in output which was
0.63 percent of the GDP from that year. Looking at the indirect impact of these
S-ESOPs, they further supported 940,000 jobs with $48 billion in income with
an average salary of $50,000. The indirect output values at $153 billion which was
1.1 percent of the GDP that year.[160] The numbers from this study were only taken
from active participants of the ESOPs so one might assume that the impact numbers are more substantial than the study concludes.

Endnotes

1.   "Types of Co-Ops," UW Center for Cooperatives, University of Wisconsin-Madison, n.d., https://uwcc.wisc.edu/about-co-ops/types-of-co-ops/.
Access date: January 2021.

2.   Oscar Perry Abello, "Closing the Funding Gap for Worker Cooperatives," Urbanist News, Next City, July 8, 2016, https://nextcity.org/urbanist-news/red-emmas-working-world-nyc-financial-cooperative. Publication date: july 8, 2016.

3.   Joseph Proudhon, quoted in Daniel Guérin, For a Libertarian Communism, ed. David Berry, trans. Mitchell Abidor (Oakland: PM Press, 2017), n.p.
The French Revolution of 1848 sparked a wave of similar revolts across Europe in what came to be known as the "Springtime of Nations."

4.   The International Workingmen's Association (IWA), founded in 1864 and disbanded in 1876, is more commonly referred to as the "First International."

5.   Karl Marx, quoted in Bruno Jossa, "Marx, Marxism and the cooperative movement," Cambridge Journal of Economics 29, no. 1 (2005): 3–18, http://www.jstor.org/stable/23603445. It should be noted that Marx was not as anti-cooperative as he appears in many of his writings.

6.   Vladimir Lenin, "On Party Unity," The Tenth Congress of the R.C.P. Verbatim Report, March 8-16, 1921, in Collected Works, ed. and trans. Yuri Sdobnikov (Moscow: Progress Publishers, 1965), https://www.marxists.org/archive/lenin/works/1921/10thcong/ch04.htm.

7.   Rosa Luxemburg, "Co-operatives, Unions, Democracy," Social Reform or Revolution (London: Militant Publications, 1986), https://www.marxists.org/archive/luxemburg/1900/reform-revolution/ch07.htm.

8.   Bruno Jossa, "Marx, Lenin and the Cooperative Movement, Review of Political Economy 26, no. 2 (2014): 299.

9.   Lewis Siegelbaum, "Cooperatives," Seventeen Moments in Soviet History, Michigan State University, n.d., accessed July 20, 2021, https://soviethistory.msu.edu/1985-2/cooperatives/.

10.   John Curl, For All the People: Uncovering the Hidden History of Cooperation, Cooperative Movements, and Communalism in America (Oakland, CA: PM Press, 2012).

11.   John Clay, "Can Union Co-Ops Help Save Democracy?" Truthout, July 4, 2013, https://truthout.org/articles/can-union-co-ops-help-save-democracy/.

12.   Eric Arnesen, "Introduction," Labor 9, no. 3 (September 2012): 25–27. Arnesen reminds readers that historians remain divided on the Knights' role in the Haymarket Riots.

13.   Curl, For All the People, 104.

14.   Bruce Laurie, Artisans into Workers (New York: Noonday, 1989), 35–37, 44-45.

15.   Curl, 32, 36. By 1825, Robert Owen—largely credited for laying the groundwork for the modern cooperative—had come to the US from the UK and established a cooperative store in New Harmony, Indiana.

16.   Jessica Gordon Nembhard, Collective Courage: A History of African American Cooperative Economic Thought and Practice (University Park, PA: Pennsylvania State University Press, 2014).

17.   Nembhard, Collective Courage.

18.   Curl, 4.

19.   Peggy Deamer, "The Sherman Antitrust Act and the Profession of Architecture," Avery Review 36 (January 2019).

20.   Curl, 119.

21.   Phil Kenkel, "Cooperatives and Anti-Trust," Cooperatives Community of Practice, National Cooperative Extension, August 21, 2019, https://cooperatives.extension.org/cooperatives-and-anti-trust/.

22.   Curl, 188.

23.   "1935 Passage of the Wagner Act," Our History, National Relations Labor Board, 2012, https://www.nlrb.gov/about-nlrb/who-we-are/our-history/1935-passage-of-the-wagner-act.

24.   In 1935, the New Deal created the Rural Electrification Administration to provide loans to local electrifications cooperatives, encouraging many such co-ops to form in rural communities. The Tennessee Valley Authority Program, created in 1933, and the Farm Securities Administration, created in 1935, also encouraged and formed many cooperatives. The 1933 Farm Credit Administration set up banks for cooperatives. Curl, 172–176, 187.

25.   Curl, 190.

26.   Foster Rhea Dulles, Labor in America, 3rd ed. (New York: Thomas Y. Crowell, 1966), 358.

27.   Christopher Wright, "ScholarWorks at UMass Boston Worker Cooperatives and Revolution: History and Possibilities in the United States" (master's thesis, University of Massachusetts Boston, 2010), https://scholarworks.umb.edu/masters_theses/19.

28.   Curl, 209–210.

29.   This trend is international. In 1996, the United Nations adopted a resolution recommending the consideration of cooperatives to meet economic and social development goals worldwide.

30.   Elizabeth Lechleitner, "Landmark Employee Ownership Act, Signed into Law Yesterday, Will Amend Lending Landscape for Worker Co-Ops," National Cooperative Business Association CLUSA, August 14, 2018, https://ncbaclusa. coop/blog/landmark-employee-ownership-act-signed-into-law-yesterday-will-amend-lending-landscape-for-worker-co-ops/.

31.   C.R.S. § 7-56-210, Renewable Energy Cooperatives, 2004 (Public Utilities, Ch. 298, 1121); C.R.S. § 7-58-101, The Colorado Uniform Limited Cooperative Association Act (ULCAA), 2011 (Corporations and Associations, Ch. 197, 761).

32.   The act consists of a series of amendments and additions proposed in an assembly bill, CA AB-816, Cooperative corporations: worker cooperatives, 2015-2016 (Corporations Code, Ch. 192). The amended sections include: CA § 1-3-12200, 12238, 12243, 12253, 12310, 12404, 12420, 12431, 12460, 12461, 12530, 12653, and 25100; the added sections include: CA § 1-3-12201.5, 12228.3, 12230.5, 12253.5, 12310.5, 12317, 12404.5, 12454.5, 12460.5, 12530.5, and 12656.5.

33.   Many more states have agricultural cooperative statutes because of antitrust protections and direct agricultural cooperative financing. Worker-cooperative statutes have been harder to generate.

34.   Clay, "Can Union Co-Ops Help Save Democracy?"

35.   Dave Zuckerman, "USW and Mondragon Unveil Union Co-Op," The Democracy Collaborative, April 13, 2012, https://community-wealth.org/content/ usw-and-mondragon-unveil-union-co-op.

Laura Hanson Schlachter, "Stronger Together? The USW-Mondragon Union Co-Op Model," Labor Studies Journal 42 no. 2 (April 27, 2017): 124–147, https:// doi.org/10.1177/0160449X17696989.

36.   "Can Unions and Cooperatives Join Forces? An Interview with United Steelworkers President Leo Gerard," Co-Ops: Resources and Updates, United Steelworkers, accessed September 2021, https://www.usw.org/union/ featured-projects/co-ops-resources-and-updates.

37.   Rebecca Lurie and Bernadette King Fitzsimons, A Union Toolkit for Cooperative Solutions (New York, NY: Partner & Partners, Autumn 2021), https://slu.cuny.edu/wp-content/uploads/2021/11/28283961_Union_Toolkit_ final_11-2021.pdf.

38.   Curl, 2.

39.   "The Mondragon Corporation in Brief," Media Kit, Mondragon Corporation, accessed 2021, https://www.mondragon-corporation.com/ wp-content/uploads/docs/MONDRAGON-media-kit-EN.pdf.

40.   Vera Negri Zamagni, interview by John Duda, "Learning from Emilia Romagna's Cooperative Economy," The Next System Project, February 18, 2016, https://thenextsystem.org/learning-from-emilia-romagna. For a more detailed explanation, see Vera Zamagni and Tito Menzani, "Cooperative Networks in the Italian economy," Enterprise and Society 11, no. 1 (March 2010): 98–127.

41.   John Duda, "The Italian Region Where Co-Ops Produce a Third of Its GDP," YES! Magazine, July 5, 2016, https://www.yesmagazine.org/economy/2016/07/05/the-italian-place-where-co-ops-drive-the-economy-and-most-people-are-members.

42.   Nembhard, Collective Courage; Ben Craig and John Pencavel, "The Behavior of Worker Cooperatives: The Plywood Companies of the Pacific Northwest," American Economic Review 82, no. 5 (December 1992): 1083–1105, https://www.jstor.org/stable/2117468.

43.   Joyce Rothschild, "Creating a Just and Democratic Workplace: More Engagement, Less Hierarchy," Contemporary Sociology 29, no. 1 (January 2000): 195–213, https://www.jstor.org/stable/2654944.

44.   Lawrence Mishel and Jori Kandra, "CEO Pay Has Skyrocketed 1,322% Since 1978: CEOs Were Paid 351 Times as Much as a Typical Worker In 2020," Economic Policy Institute, August 10, 2021, https://www.epi.org/publication/ceo-pay-in-2020/; see also David Gelles, "C.E.O. Pay Remains Stratospheric, Even at Companies Battered by Pandemic," New York Times, April 24, 2021, https://www.nytimes.com/2021/04/24/business/ceos-pandemic-compensation.html.

45.   E. G. Nadeau, The Cooperative Solution: How the United States Can Tame Recessions, Reduce Inequality, and Protect the Environment (CreateSpace Independent Publishing Platform, July 26, 2012), 5; see also Gabriel Burdín and Andrés Dean, "New Evidence on Wages and Employment in Worker Cooperatives Compared with Capitalist Firms," Journal of Comparative Economics 37, no. 4 (December 2009): 517–533.

46.   Nembhard, Collective Courage; Rothschild, "Creating a Just and Democratic Workplace," 202.

47.   Kermit Baker, Jessica Mentz, Jennifer Riskus, and Michele Russo, "The Business of Architecture 2020: Firm Survey Report" (Washington, DC: The American Institute of Architects, 2020), 11. The acronym BIPOC, which stands for Black, Indigenous, and people of color, is replaced by the phrase "members of a racially and/or ethnically diverse demographic group" in the AIA Firm Survey Report.

48.   Randy Hodson, Working with Dignity (Cambridge: Cambridge University Press, 2000), cited in Rothschild, "Creating a Just and Democratic Workplace," 195.

49.   Mary N. Woods, From Craft to Profession: The Practice of Architecture in Nineteenth-Century America (Berkeley, CA: University of California Press, 1999), 5

50.   David Brain, "Practical Knowledge and Occupational Control: The Professionalization of Architecture in the United States," Sociological Forum 6, no. 2 (1991): 239–268, https://doi.org/10.1007/bf01114392. Brain frames the practice of architecture in the US during the eighteenth century as "a body of knowledge associated with cultivated taste. It was not yet identified with a distinct occupational practice, nor was there a framework within which the authorial contribution of a designer could be distinguished," 242.

51.   Woods, From Craft to Profession, 12.

52.   Woods, 9.

53.   Brain, "Practical Knowledge and Occupational Control," 242; Woods, 14.

54.   Brain, 242–244.

55.   Ibid., 244.

56.   Many US architects studied at the École des Beaux-Arts in Paris, France. Beyond formal education, exposure to a multitude of styles of architecture was considered essential knowledge. See Dana Cuff, Architecture: The Story of Practice (Cambridge, MA: The MIT Press, 1996[1992]), 25–26. Brain notes that "the first self-consciously 'professional' architects began their careers as draftsmen in the few architectural offices in existence in the first part of the [eighteenth] century, obtaining these positions on the basis of business and family connections." Brain, 245.

57.   Cuff, Architecture, 23.

58.   Some US men who studied at the École des Beaux-Arts were dedicated to passing along their education to their apprentices for the "improvement of the profession." See Henry H. Saylor, "The A-I-A-'s First Hundred Years," (May 1957): 110–111.

59.   This language is retained in the Intern Development Program (IDP) within the architecture licensing process. Interns are required to have their hours metered and approved by a "mentor" who is a licensed architect.

60.   Saylor, "The A-I-A-'s First Hundred Years," 13.

61.   There were two tiers of members in the early days of the profession: professional members or fellows were highly regarded by the membership, while associates were "paternally regarded as children." To become a member an architect had to become a candidate, proposed by two current members, discussed in the "Rooms" for thirty days, and finally voted on by professional members (associates were disenfranchised). Three no votes meant the candidate was disqualified from membership. To graduate from an associate to professional member required a vote by the Board of Trustees. This arduous and exclusive process kept membership very low for the first one hundred years of the organization. Saylor, 14, 29–30.

62.   Cuff, 26.

63.   Cuff cites Laron's discussion of the impact of professionalization in architecture, 23–57.

64.   Saylor, 110.

65.   Ibid., 109.

66.   Ibid., 114.

67.   "Beginning of Licensure," National Council of Architecture Registration Boards (NCARB), accessed October 2020, https://centennial.ncarb.org/beginning-of-licensure/.

68.   The National Council of Architectural Registration Boards (NCARB) was established in 1919 due to the need for reciprocity in licensure and registration between states. The first licensing exams were developed in 1921, and continued with no substantial change until 1965. See "Beginning of Licensure," https://centennial.ncarb.org/beginning-of-licensure/.

69.   Saylor, 34.

70.   Quoted from a report issued by the Education Committee of the AIA (architect Ralph Adams Cram, chairman), cited in Saylor, 39.

71.   This was not dissimilar to the medical profession's distinction between physicians and "irregulars," however, the regulation of licensure within the medical profession was more ad hoc: "by the end of the civil war not a single state was attempting to regulate the practice of medicine." John F. Duffy, From Humors to Medical Science: A History of American Medicine (Chicago, IL: University of Chicago Press, 1993), 141.

72.   Saylor, 30.

73.   Laura, Gottesman, "Research Guides: Great Depression and New Deal: A General Resource Guide: Introduction," Library of Congress, accessed October 2021, https://www.loc.gov/rr/program/bib/newdeal/habs.html.

74.   David E. Lilienthal, TVA: Democracy on the March (New York: Harper & Brothers, 1953).

75.   Peggy Deamer, "The Sherman Antitrust Act and the Profession of Architecture," Avery Review 36 (January 2019), https://www.averyreview.com/issues/36/sherman-antitrust-act.

76.   Curl, 244. In 1981, President Ronald Reagan's incoming administration responded to a coincidental recession by offering tax cuts to large corporations, reducing government regulations, privatizing or slashing spending on social programs, and allocating additional money to the military. By 1989, the end of Reagan's second term, unions were weakened, and many of the cooperatives supported by the boom social movements of the 1960s and '70s ceased to exist.

77.   The issue was considered by the Supreme Court in 1978: National Society of Professional Engineers, Petitioner, v. United States, 435 U.S. 679 (1978).

See Barry Wasserman, Patrick J. Sullivan, and Gregory Palermo, *Ethics and Practice of Architecture* (New York: John Wiley & Sons, 2000), 115.

78.   Ibid. Prior to this, the AIA maintained a suggested fee schedule (one of many throughout its history), prohibited members from discounting fees, and through its code of ethics prevented members from engaging in competitive behavior.

United States v The American Institute of Architects, Civil Action No. 992-72, 1972 as relayed in Deamer, "The Sherman Antitrust Act and the Profession of Architecture."

79.   National Society of Professional Engineers v. United States [435 US 679], 692 (1978)

80.   Aram Mardirosian, who had been stripped of AIA membership for violation of the supplanting rule, Standard 9, successfully challenged the AIA. See Deamer, "The Sherman Antitrust Act and the Profession of Architecture." Following the ruling, the AIA replaced its Code of Ethics with a Statement of Voluntary Ethical Principles. A new Code of Ethics was reintroduced in 1987.

81.   Peggy Deamer gives examples of the decree's effect: "two architects agreeing to boycott an architectural competition is illegal; architects in a local area agreeing to not submit an RFP for a certain project is illegal." Deamer, "The Sherman Antitrust Act and the Profession of Architecture."

82.   Taylorization is a form of "scientific management," described by Frederick Taylor, which seeks to divide work into discrete tasks for the purpose of greater efficiency and productivity. The practice also reinforces neat and well-defined hierarchies within offices; such division of tasks is standard practice within large architectural offices.

83.   Baker, Mentz, Riskus, and Russo, "The Business of Architecture 2020: Firm Survey Report," 8.

84.   Ibid., 51.

85.   Ibid., 44. Most firms with 20 or fewer employees were founded as recently as the 1990s or since.

86.   Ibid., 25, 64.

87.   The first Firm Survey Report was published in 1979, but no copy of this edition exists in the AIA archive.

88.   One such overlooked malpractice is the ever-common unpaid internship that propagates the "dues paying" myth among younger staff, which in turn leads to low starting wages in proportion to an architecture student's typical school debt. Other common labor malpractices include required unpaid overtime and toxic work environments. See Audrey Wachs, "What is going on at SCI-Arc?" *Architect's Newspaper*, March 31, 2022, https://www.archpaper.com/2022/03/what-is-going-on-at-sci-arc/; Dank Lloyd Wright, "We Could All Be Less Complicit," Architecture, Workplace, e-flux, November 2021,

https://www.e-flux.com/architecture/workplace/430302/
we-could-all-be-less-complicit/.

89.   Trevor Young-Hyman, Nathalie Magne, and Douglas L. Kruse, "A Real
Utopia Under What Conditions? The Economic and Social Benefits of Workplace
Democracy in Knowledge-Intensive Industries," Social Science Research
Network, July 7, 2022, http://dx.doi.org/10.2139/ssrn.4147748.

90.   These groups were also organized for the benefit of the public good. In the
case of the Associated Architects of Los Angeles, shared profits were "applied to
educational or other works to advance the cause of architecture." See "The Fifty-
Sixth Convention of the A.I.A.," Architectural Forum, June 1923, 311–312. The
bylaws of the Allied Architects of Washington, DC, "provided for one-fourth of
the corporation's net proceeds to be spent on efforts to advance architecture in
the District of Columbia and to educate the public about good design." DC Office
of Planning, DC Architect's Directory, October 2010, https://planning.dc.gov/
sites/default/files/dc/sites/op/publication/attachments/Architects 20Bios%20
A%20and%20B.pdf.

91.   The AIA eventually reversed this position but required collective
organizations to meet with them annually in order to review intent and methods,
and determine if they would be allowed to continue. Saylor, 62.

92.   Ibid.

93.   Ibid., 63. The office of the supervising architect was founded in 1852
 when the profession was still in its infancy. See "Architecture and Government,"
US General Services Administration, accessed December 2021,
https://www.gsa.gov/real-estate/historic-preservation/
historic-building-stewardship/architecture-and-government.

94.   Saylor, 63.

95.   Ibid., 38.

96.   "Architects Draft Code of Practice," New York Times, August 7, 1933: 25,
as quoted in Mardges Bacon, "The Federation of Architects, Engineers,
Chemists and Technicians (FAECT): The Politics and Social Practice of Labor,"
Journal of the Society of Architectural Historians 76, no. 4 (December 2017): 454.

97.   Draftsmen were granted AIA membership in 1900 if they had been
employed by a fellow for five years or more and were recommended by three
additional fellows. Saylor, 36.

98.   Bacon, "The Federation of Architects, Engineers, Chemists and Technicians
(FAECT)," 454.

99.   "FAECT Four Years Old!" FAECT Bulletin 4 (September 1937), 10, as cited
in Bacon, 455.

100.   Tony Schuman, "Professionalization and the Social Goals of Architects:
A History of the Federation of Architects, Engineers, Chemists and Technicians,"

in The Design Professions and the Built Environment, ed. Paul L. Knox
(New York: Nichols, 1988), 12–41.

101.   Bacon, 458–459.

102.   Eventually, FAECT helped pass the Wagner-Steagall Housing Bill
(the Housing Act of 1937) which created the US Housing Authority within the
Department of the Interior. Even with this success, there is evidence that FAECT
wanted the bill to be even more progressive, citing that the bill's "elimination
of loans to alternative implementation agencies ... such as labor unions, nonprofit
housing societies, cooperatives, and limited-dividend societies" was "a serious
blow." D. Bradford Hunt, "Was the 1937 US Housing Act a Pyrrhic Victory?"
Journal of Planning History 4, no. 3 (2005), 205.

103.   Martin Dies, "The Federation of Architects, Engineers, Chemists,
and Technicians—A Story of Communist Infiltration into the Foundations
of the National-Defense Program," 87 Congressional Record, 1941, A1301,
cited in Bacon, 461. FAECT included technical workers in US defense industries
such as naval construction, which involved national security.

104.   Bacon, 461.

105.   The disposition of architects towards design runs counter to such
requests. As Andrew Brodie Smith writes, "to ask an architect not to specify
a particular brand of building product would be like asking physicians not to
dispense a much-needed medication." Brodie Smith, "UAW President Bathed
in Applause at the AIA Centennial Convention," AIArchitect, January 2006,
http://info.aia.org/aiarchitect/thisweek06/0113/a150_two11306.htm.

106.   Doug Michels, "Interview with Ant Farm," in Constance M. Lewallen
and Steve Seid, Ant Farm 1968–1978 (Berkeley, CA: University of California
Press, 2004), 41.

107.   David Maulen, "The Integral Architect: Co-Op design in Chile,"
Bauhaus Magazine 7 (2015): 95, 99.

108.   "Archigram: The True Story Told by Peter Cook," The Story of Archigram,
Archigram, accessed February 2022, https://www.archigram.net/story.html.

109.   James Imam, "Architects Dreaming of a Future with No Buildings,"
New York Times, February 12, 2021, https://www.nytimes.com/2021/02/12/arts/
design/superstudio-civa.html.

110.   Zoya Gul Hasan, "'We Dream of Instant Cities That Could Sprout
like Spring Flowers': The Radical Architecture Collectives of the 60s and 70s,"
ArchDaily, January 16, 2019, accessed February 2022, https://www.archdaily.
com/880253/9-of-the-most-bizarre-and-forward-thinking-radical-architecture-
groups-of-the-60s-and-70s.

111.   Michael Kubo, "Collaborative Tasks," Log 48: Expanding Modes of Practice
no. 48, (Winter/Spring 2020): 81–92.

112.   Kubo, "Collaborative Tasks," 90–91.

113.   "Architects in the US - Number of Businesses 2003–2028," Industry Statistics - United States, IBISWorld, accessed 2021, https://www.ibisworld.com/industry-statistics/number-of-businesses/architects-united-states/.

114.   Gabriel Cira, Peggy Deamer, Ashton Hamm, James Heard, Will Martin, Quilian Riano, Shawhin Roudbari, and Christian Rutherford, "Template for a Cooperative Network of Small Architecture Practices," MAS Context, August 12, 2020, https://mascontext.com/observations/template-for-a-cooperative-network-of-small-architecture-practices/#1a.

115.   Ibid.

116.   Ibid.

117.   "Membership & Insurance," ArchiTeam, accessed 2021, https://www.architeam.net.au/membership/insurance.

118.   In the past five years there have been strides towards unionization among architects. Early in 2022, SHoP employees made an attempt to unionize but ultimately backed away from these efforts. Later that year, the first private architecture union was founded at Bernheimer Architecture in New York City. See Noam Scheiber, "Architects at a Prominent New York Firm Drop Their Unionization Bid." New York Times, February 4, 2022, https://www.nytimes.com/2022/02/04/business/economy/shop-architects-union.html; Noam Scheiber, "Architects at a New York Firm Form the Industry's Only Private-Sector Union." New York Times, September 1, 2022, https://www.nytimes.com/2022/09/01/business/architects-union.html.

119.   Baker et. al., "The Business of Architecture 2020," 45.

120.   "Baby Boomers: Incredible Numbers Buying and Selling," Home, California Association of Business Brokers, accessed 2021, https://cabb.org/selling-a-business-in-ca/baby-boomers-incredible-numbers-buying-and-selling.

121.   With the looming market surge of private businesses for sale, the number of private businesses that actually sell will drop far below 20 percent. See Lori Shepherd, "Why an Increasing Number of Retiring Entrepreneurs Are Selling the Business to Their Employees," Entrepreneur, February 21, 2018, https://www.entrepreneur.com/article/308785.

122.   In October 2021, Foster + Partners' management choose to sell the company to a Canadian investment firm rather than its workers. The firm has 180 partners and 1,500 employees spanning their 14 offices. While Foster + Partners has made it clear that there will be no change in operations because of this sale, it is surely a missed opportunity for workers to gain any control within the company.

123.   There are several names for this movement: the Just Transition, the Solidarity Economy, the Sustainable Economy, etc.; all look to support democratic, sustainable, and equitable alternatives to capitalism.

124.   "Cooperative Identity, Values & Principles," International Cooperative Alliance, last modified 2016, https://www.ica.coop/en/cooperatives/cooperative-identity. The founders of the International Cooperative Alliance (ICA), based in Belgium, reviewed the core values and principles of the Rochdale Society which had guided its organization for fifty years. These principles were formally adopted by the ICA, and have become standard tenets for cooperatives internationally.

125.   2021 State of the Sector: Worker Cooperatives in the US, Democracy at Work Institute, US Federation of Worker Cooperatives, January 2022, https://institute.coop/resources/2021-worker-cooperative-state-sector-report.

126.   "Cooperative Identity, Values & Principles," International Cooperative Alliance, 2016.

127.   Think Outside the Boss: How to Create Worker Owned Businesses, 3rd ed., Sustainable Economies Law Center, Democary at Work Institute (March 2013), 2, https://institute.coop/sites/default/files/resources/SELC%20-%20 Think%20Outside%20the%20Boss.pdf

128.   Choosing a Business Entity: A Guide for Worker Cooperatives, US Federation of Worker Cooperatives, Democracy at Work Institute, n.d., https://institute.coop/sites/default/files/ChoicofEntityFinal.pdf.

129.   Think Outside the Boss, Sustainable Economies Law Center, 14. https://institute.coop/sites/default/files/resources/SELC%20-%20Think%20 Outside%20the%20Boss.pdf

130.   Meegan Moriarty, "USDA Cooperative Legislation Spreadsheet," United States Department of Agriculture (unpublished document, accessed in 2020), Excel file.

131.   Uniform state laws denote an effort to standardize certain statutory laws between states. This has become increasingly necessary as interstate commerce and business has developed. The Uniform Law Commission, comprised of over 300 commissioners across all 50 states, reviews, recommends, and adopts these uniform laws. See "Uniform Laws," Legal Information Institute, Cornell Law School, https://www.law.cornell.edu/uniform; and "About Us," Uniform Law Commission, https://www.uniformlaws.org/aboutulc/overview.

132.   "Limited Cooperative Association Act—Enactment Map," Uniform Law Commission, 2007, https://www.uniformlaws.org/committees/ community-home?CommunityKey=22f0235d-9d23-4fe0-ba9e-10f02ae0bfd0.

133.   "Colorado—The Delaware of Cooperative Law" is a registered trademark of Jason Weiner, PC, a Public Benefit Corporation, 2020. Litigator and activist Jason Weiner was a great help in describing the suite of cooperative legislation that the state offers. Phone call with author, February, 2021.

134.   Jane Haskins, "What Are Articles of Incorporation?" Business Formation, Legal Zoom, accessed 2022, https://www.legalzoom.com/articles/ articles-of-incorporation-what-are-articles-of-incorporation.

135.   Some entity types—S Corporations, for example—may only have one class of owners.

136.   Galen Rapp and Gerald Ely, How to Start a Cooperative, Cooperative Information Report 7, United States Department of Agriculture, Rural Development: Business and Cooperative Programs, revised by James J. Wadsworth, 2015 (September 1996), https://www.rd.usda.gov/files/publications/ CIR 207%20How%20to%20Start%20a%20Cooperative%20%282015%29.pdf.

137.   See glossary for an explanation of these terms.

138.   This information comes thanks to the Sustainable Economies Law Center's webinar, "Subchapter T & How Money Flows Through a Cooperative," and to various conversations with CPAs over the years. See Ricardo Nuñez and Gregory Jackson, "Teach-In: How Money Flows," Sustainable Economies Law Center and The City of Berkeley's Office of Economic Development, 2021, https://www.youtube.com/watch?v=vgvoxxwnyqU.

139.   It should be noted that fees for attorneys and tax professions can be cost prohibitive. However, some attorneys within the co-op community will work pro bono. See appendix.

140.   This applies to "ordinary" rather than "qualified" dividends, which are taxed at the lower corporate capital gains rate.

141.   "Facts About the Qualified Business Income Deduction," New Releases, FS-2019-8, Internal Revenue Service, April 2019, https://www.irs.gov/newsroom/ facts-about-the-qualified-business-income-deduction.

142.   26 US Code §1388 gives the legal definition of businesses operating on a cooperative basis for the purpose of the tax code. 26 US Code §1381(a)(2) applies specifically to T Corporations.

143.   The case of Puget Sound Plywood, Inc. v. Commissioner, 44 T.C. 305 (1965) set the standards by which the IRS defines T Corporations. See "Case Law and Administrative Rulings," Resource Library, Co-OpLaw.org, accessed 2021, https://www.co-oplaw.org/knowledge-base/caselaw/.

144.   Design Anarchy Cooperative used this strategy to incorporate in Colorado and while doing business in Indiana. See https://www.anarchy.coop.

145.   Baker et. al., "The Business of Architecture 2020," 45.

146.   Brett Heeger, Esq., of Gundzik, Gundzik, Heeger, LLP, developed this idea. See Heeger et al.,

"Community Capital Raising Workbook," Sustainable Economies Law Center, (forthcoming 2022).

147.   Camille Kerr and Joe Rinehart, Becoming Employee Owned, Cooperative Ownership Transitions, Democracy at Work Institute, US Federation of Worker Cooperatives, 2014, https://institute.coop/sites/default/files/resources/ COT_BecomingEmployeeOwned_FINALweb.pdf.

148.   Camille Kerr, A Brief, Visual Guide to Understanding Employee Ownership Structures, Democracy at Work Institute, US Federation of Worker Cooperatives, n.d., https://institute.coop/sites/default/files/resources/EOStructures.pdf. Access date: July 2021.

149.   John Abrams and William Greider, Companies We Keep: Employee Ownership and the Business of Community and Place (White River Junction, Vermont: Chelsea Green Publishing, 2008).

150.   Galen Rapp and Gerald Ely, How to Start a Cooperative, Cooperative Information Report 7, United States Department of Agriculture, Rural Development: Business and Cooperative Programs, revised by James J. Wadsworth, 2015 (September 1996).

151.   Rebecca Lurie and Bernadette King Fitzsimons, A Union Toolkit for Cooperative Solutions, The Community and Worker Ownership Project at the CUNY School of Labor and Urban Studies (New York: Partner & Partners, Autumn 2021), https://slu.cuny.edu/wp-content/uploads/2021/11/28283961_Union_Toolkit_final_11-2021.pdf.

152.   "Our Story," New Era Windows Cooperative, accessed January 2022, https://www.newerawindows.com/Content/our-story.html.

153.   Jaques Kaswan, Projecting the Long-Term Consequences of ESOP vs CO-OP Conversion of a Firm on Employee Benefits and Company Cash, Research Report 5, University of California Davis Center for Cooperatives, Democratic Business Association of Northern California, May 1992.

154.   The transition to an ESOP requires owners to sell a some or all of their shares to the ESOP trust, which may require a loan. See Camille Kerr and Joe Rinehart, Becoming Employee Owned: Options for Business Owners Interested in Engaging Employees Through Ownership, Cooperative Ownership Transitions, Democracy at Work Institute, 2014, https://institute.coop/sites/default/files/resources/COT_BecomingEmployeeOwned_FINALweb.pdf.

155.   A non-leveraged ESOP does not borrow funds for its creation, rather it is funded by contributions of cash or stock directly from the employee-sponsor. A leveraged ESOP uses a financial institution, or a lender, to either acquire new shares issued by the employer or purchase shares from a selling shareholder.

156.   Madeline Liu, "The Tax Benefits of Employee Stock Ownership Plans," Harris CPAs, last modified December 18, 2019, https://harriscpas.com/the-tax-benefits-of-employee-stock-ownership-plans/.

157.   See "Employee Ownership by the Numbers," National Center for Employee Ownership, December 2021, https://www.nceo.org/articles/employee-owner-ship-by-the-numbers#1; 2021 State of the Sector: Worker Cooperatives in the US, Democracy at Work Institute, US Federation of Worker Cooperatives, January 2022, https://institute.coop/resources/2021-worker-cooperative-state-sector-report.

158.   Philip Reeves and Todd Leverette, "Black and Brown Employee Ownership for the Post-COVID Economy,"

Democracy and Power, ImpactAlpha, June 10, 2020, https://impactalpha.com/black-and-brown-employee-ownership-for-the-post-covid-economy/.

159.   "The Employee Ownership 100: America's Largest Majority Employee-Owned Companies," National Center for Employee Ownership, last modified November 1, 2022, https://www.nceo.org/articles/employee-ownership-100.

160.   Alex Brill, Macroeconomic Impact of S ESOPs on the U.S. Economy, Matrix Global Advisors, White Paper, April 17, 2013, https://esca.us/wp-content/uploads/2021/07/Macroecomic_Impact_of_S_ESOPs_study_4_17_13.pdf.

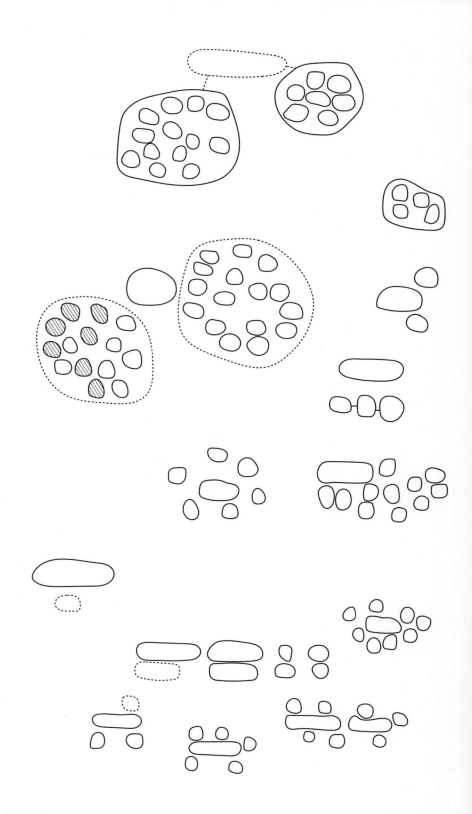

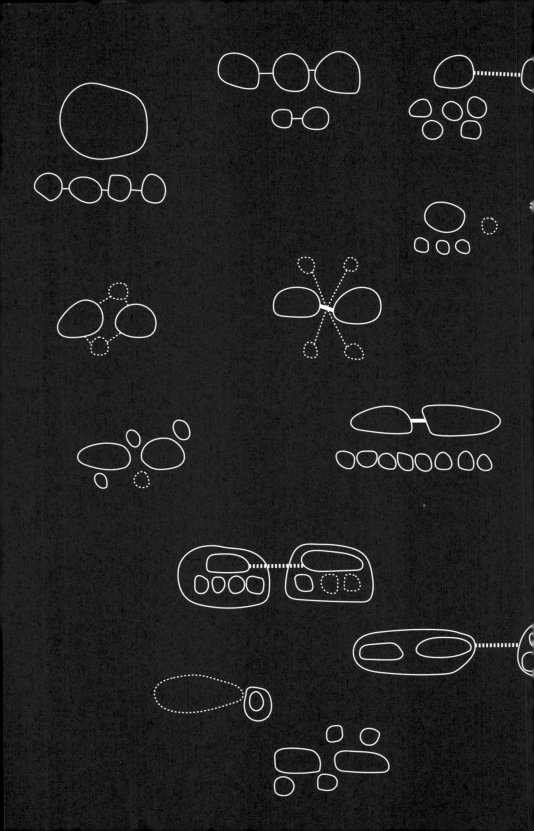

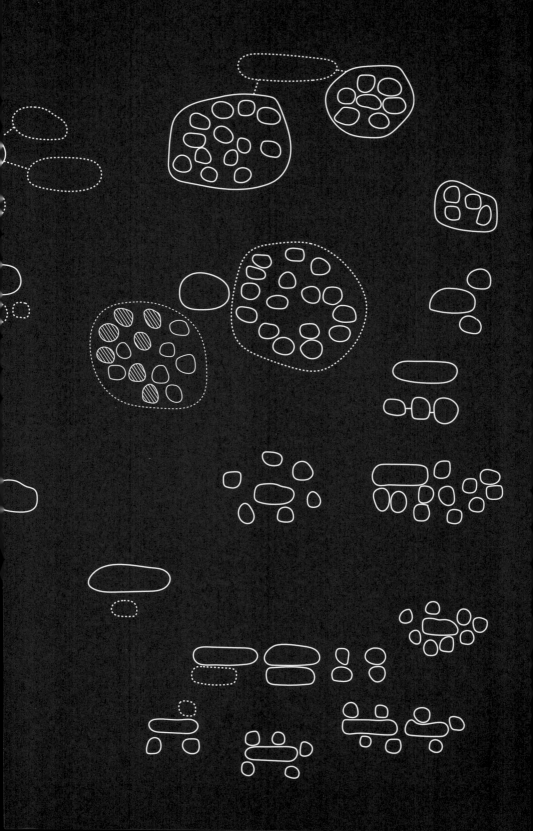

ORO Editions
Publishers of Architecture, Art, and Design
Gordon Goff: Publisher

www.oroeditions.com
info@oroeditions.com

Published by ORO Editions.

Author: Ashton Hamm
Book Design: Pablo Mandel / CircularStudio
Project Manager: Jake Anderson

10 9 8 7 6 5 4 3 2 1 FIRST EDITION

ISBN: 978-1-951541-95-8

Color Separations and Printing: ORO Group Inc.
Printed in China

ORO Editions makes a continuous effort to minimize the
overall carbon footprint of its publications. As part of this
goal, ORO, in association with Global ReLeaf, arranges
to plant trees to replace those used in the manufacturing
of the paper produced for its books. Global ReLeaf is an
international campaign run by American Forests, one
of the world's oldest nonprofit conservation organizations.
Global ReLeaf is American Forests' education and action
program that helps individuals, organizations, agencies,
and corporations improve the local and global environment
by planting and caring for trees.